Answering
MORMONS'
Questions

Cult Resources
From Bethany House Publishers

Mormonism
> *Answering Mormons' Questions*—McKeever
> *How to Answer a Mormon*—Morey
> *Letters to a Mormon Elder*—White
> *Mormonism*—Martin
> *Questions to Ask Your Mormon Friend*—McKeever/Johnson
> *Thirty Questions to Ask Your Mormon Friend*—McKeever

Jehovah's Witnesses
> *How to Answer a Jehovah's Witness*—Morey
> *Jehovah of the Watchtower*—Martin
> *Watchtower Files*—Magnani/Barrett

Occult and Astrology
> *Demon Possession*—Montgomery
> *Horoscopes and the Christian*—Morey
> *Principalities and Powers*—Montgomery

New Age and Eastern Religions
> *Baha'i*—Beckwith
> *New Age Cult*—Martin
> *A Reasoned Look at Asian Religions*—Johnson
> *Reincarnation and Christianity*—Morey

Others
> *Christian Science*—Martin
> *Herbert Armstrong*—Martin
> *Sun Myung Moon and the Unification Church*—Bjornstad

General
> *Building Your Christian Defense System*—Niquette
> *The Kingdom of the Cults*—Martin

Answering
MORMONS'
Questions
Bill McKeever

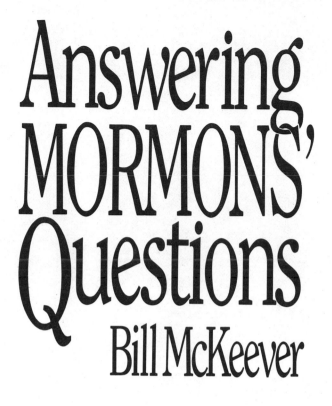

BETHANY HOUSE PUBLISHERS
MINNEAPOLIS, MINNESOTA 55438

Published by Bethany House Publishers
A Ministry of Bethany Fellowship, Inc.
6820 Auto Club Road, Minneapolis, Minnesota 55438

Printed in the United States of America

Library of Congress Cataloging-in-Publication Data

McKeever, Bill
    Answering Mormons' questions / Bill McKeever.
        p. cm.
    Includes bibliographical references and index.

    1. Church of Jesus Christ of Latter-Day Saints—Controversial
literature. 2. Mormon Church—Controversial literature. I. Title.
BX8645.M395   1991
289.3—dc20   90–24039
ISBN 1–55661–201–X   CIP

I would like to thank all my Christian brothers and sisters who have kept me, my family, and this ministry before the Lord in prayer. I also wish to thank Eric Johnson and Dave Costantino, two close brothers in Christ, for their help in preparing this manuscript for print.

A special thanks goes to my dear wife for being patient with me while my eyes were glued to the computer screen. Thanks, Tam, you're the best.

But sanctify the Lord God in your hearts: and be ready always to give an answer to every man that asketh you a reason of the hope that is in you with meekness and fear.

1 PETER 3:15

Study to show thyself approved unto God, a workman that needeth not to be ashamed, rightly dividing the word of truth.

2 TIMOTHY 2:15

BILL McKEEVER is the founder/director of Mormonism Research Ministry, a Christian outreach organized in 1979. His study on the doctrines of Mormonism started in 1973, when he recognized his need to put his trust in Jesus Christ as Lord and Savior. Having had many friends who were Latter-day Saints, he was curious about their beliefs and began researching their fascinating religion.

Mr. McKeever's firm but compassionate manner has made him a much sought after speaker for churches, colleges, and seminaries. Along with *Answering Mormons' Questions*, he has written many other tracts and booklets on Mormonism, including the popular tract *They Come on Bicycles*. He is also editor of the magazine *Mormonism Researched*.

Bill and his wife Tamar have three children—Kristen, Kendra, and Jamin—and reside in the San Diego area.

If you would like to receive a free subscription to
Mormonism Researched,
the official publication of
Mormonism Research Ministry, write:
Mormonism Research Ministry
Dept. B
PO Box 20705
El Cajon, CA 92021

Contents

Introduction

On April 6, 1830, a new church was organized which would come to be called the Church of Jesus Christ of Latter-day Saints. Its leader was a young man who, ten years previously at the age of fourteen, had claimed to have had a vision of God the Father and Jesus Christ. His name was Joseph Smith.

According to his testimony, he was told in this vision that all churches were wrong and that he should join none of them. He was informed that all their creeds were an abomination in God's sight and that their ministers were corrupt.

Three years later, in 1823, he claimed he was visited by an angel named Moroni. In this vision he was told of a book written on gold plates that gave an account of the former inhabitants of the American continent, and "the source from whence they sprang." Also included on these plates was what the angel called "the fullness of the everlasting gospel."

These plates were buried in a hill not far from where Smith lived, but it wasn't until 1827 that he was finally given permission by the angel to retrieve them.

Also buried were "two stones in silver bows, fastened to a breastplate," which he called the Urim and Thummim. Since the plates were written in a language called "Reformed Egyptian," the Urim and Thummim would help him translate them.

In 1830 the English translation was printed as the *Book of Mormon*. It contains the story of a group of Jews led by a man named Lehi, who sailed to the Western Hemisphere from Jerusalem around 600 B.C. Lehi had two sons, Nephi and Laman. These two had a fierce argument, dividing the people. Since Laman was wrong, God showed His displeasure by darkening his skin. His dark-skinned descendants became known as Lamanites.

Years later, the hatred between these two groups erupted into a battle that annihilated all the followers of Nephi—the Nephites. Before all was lost, the leader of the Nephites, whose name was Mormon, gathered the records of his people and instructed his son Moroni to bury them. Moroni buried them on a small hill called Cumorah, and fifteen hundred years later, Joseph Smith found them there.

Smith's "ministry" would be short-lived, lasting only fourteen years after his church was organized. Although the Mormon church claims that the persecution they and their leader received was for the cause of truth, documents show us it was Smith's bungling inconsistencies and erratic behavior that eventually led to his early demise.

His teachings created many enemies, some of whom started a newspaper called the *Nauvoo Expositor*. Though only one edition was printed, it denounced the Mormon prophet. Smith ordered the printing press destroyed.

Joseph Smith, Jr.

Joseph Smith, Jr., claimed he had seen God the Father and Jesus Christ, and was told by these personages that all the churches were wrong. Smith claimed that true Christianity had been lost and that God had called him to restore the true church. To this day the Mormon church claims all other churches are in a state of apostasy.

For inciting the destruction of the newspaper office, he was incarcerated at the jail in Carthage, Illinois. The jail was attacked by an angry mob. Smith, with a smuggled pistol, killed two people and wounded another before he was killed. The church presents him as an innocent martyr.

After his death at the Carthage jail, a power struggle developed between the saints, and splinter groups were formed. Many followed Brigham Young, who led his followers to the Salt Lake Valley and became their second prophet and president.

His group, with its headquarters in Salt Lake City, Utah, retained the nickname "Mormons" and has grown to be the most powerful of all the Latter-day Saint movements. Although some things in this book may apply to one or more of the many other schisms claiming Joseph Smith as their prophet, this is the group I am writing about.

Joseph Fielding Smith, the tenth prophet and president of the Mormon church stated:

Mormonism, as it is called, must stand or fall on the story of Joseph Smith. He was either a prophet of God, divinely called, properly appointed and commissioned, or he was one of the biggest frauds this world has ever seen. There is no middle ground.

If Joseph Smith was a deceiver, who willfully attempted to mislead the people, then he should be exposed; his claims should be refuted, and his doctrines shown to be false, for the doctrines of an imposter cannot be made to harmonize in all particulars with divine truth. If his claims and declarations were built upon fraud and deceit, there would appear many errors and contradictions, which would be easy to detect. The doctrines of false teachers will not stand the test when tried by the accepted standards of measurement, the Scriptures. (*Doctrines of Salvation*, 1:188)

The purpose of this book is to accept Mr. Smith's challenge concerning the founder of his church and the doctrine he taught. We will scrutinize the teachings of Joseph Smith using the accepted standard of measurement, the Bible.

It is out of a deep love and concern for my Christian and Mormon friends that I spent hours in research to write this book. Too many souls have fallen prey to the misinterpreted scriptures brought forth by either the Mormon missionary or Mormon acquaintances.

Unlike the *Book of Mormon*, which needs other books to explain its contents, the Bible speaks for itself. I do not intend in any way to say that the explanations contained in this book are the only interpretations (there are some subjects and verses upon which one cannot be dogmatic); however, when the Bible is used as its own defense, there is no way the Mormon interpretation can be taken as reliable.

I love the Mormon people. But as sincere as they are, I honestly feel that they are *sincerely* wrong in the light of Scripture.

I pray the contents of this book will be used to strengthen the faith of every true believer, and at the same time enlighten those lost in the Mormon system who have eyes to see, ears to hear, and minds to reason.

We never criticize other churches and their beliefs.
Why do you pick on the Mormon church and what it
believes?

To say the Mormon church has never made an attempt to discredit Bible-believing people and Christianity as a whole is utterly false.

Joseph Smith attacked the Christian church, so any Christian who speaks against the Mormon system is merely defending himself and the church on the basis of the admonition in Jude 3 that tells the believer to "earnestly contend for the faith."

Joseph Smith wrote that there had been a revival in the area where he lived in New York during his boyhood in 1820. This "religious excitement," as he called it, involved the Baptist, Methodist, and Presbyterian churches. Since he was confused about which church to join, he went to the woods to pray about the matter.

Returning from the woods, he proclaimed he had actually seen God the Father and Jesus Christ standing in the air above him. When he inquired of these personages which church was true, this was the reply:

> I was answered that I must join none of them, for they were all wrong; and the Personage who addressed me said that all their creeds were an abomination in his sight; that those professors were all corrupt; that: "they draw near to me with their lips, but their hearts are far from me, they teach for doctrines the commandments of men, having a form of godliness, but they deny the power thereof." (*The Testimony of Joseph Smith*, 2:19)

Smith was not the only one with this thought concerning Christianity. Brigham Young, the second president of the Church of Jesus Christ of Latter-day Saints (LDS), said:

> The Christian world, so called, are heathens as to their knowledge of the salvation of God. (*Journal of Discourses*, 8:171)

He also stated,

With regard to true theology, a more ignorant people never lived than the present so-called Christian world. (*Journal of Discourses*, 8:199)

John Taylor, who succeeded Brigham Young as president of the Mormon church after Young's death in 1877, made these comments concerning Christianity:

We talk about Christianity, but it is a perfect pack of nonsense . . . the Devil could not invent a better engine to spread his work than the Christianity of the nineteenth century. (*Journal of Discourses*, 6:167)
What! Are Christians ignorant? Yes, as ignorant of the things of God as the brute beast. (*Journal of Discourses*, 6:25)
What does the Christian world know about God? Nothing . . . Why, so far as the things of God are concerned, they are the veriest fools; they know neither God nor the things of God. (*Journal of Discourses*, 13:225)

Orson Pratt, a Mormon apostle, made the following statement in his book *The Seer*:

All other churches are entirely destitute of all authority from God; and any person who receives Baptism, or the Lord's Supper from their hands will highly offend God, for he looks upon them as the most corrupt of all people (p. 255).

Until April 1990, the most blatant criticisms and mockeries against Christianity were found in their temple ceremony. The temple ceremony included a dialogue between a character playing the part of Lucifer and a man described as a preacher. In their first meeting Lucifer asks if the man preaches the "orthodox religion," to which the preacher answers proudly, "Yes." Lucifer then says, "If you will preach your orthodox religion to these people and convert them, I will pay you well." To this the preacher answers enthusiastically, "I will do my best."

Later on in the dialogue it becomes clear that this *orthodox religion* considered to be heresy by Mormons is really the faith held dear by many Bible-believing Christians. The doctrines of God dwelling in a believer's heart, of a hell with fire and flames, and the biblical principle that men are saved by the grace of God without any act on the part of man are all ridiculed.

The Christian preacher was portrayed as a fool who had no idea whom he was speaking to until Lucifer revealed himself later on in the ceremony.

It is not true that Mormonism does not attack Christianity. Its very tenets are an affront to Christianity as a whole, since they believe the work of Christ was not enough to save man. The Mormon believes Christ died and rose again merely to pave the way for all men to be resurrected. Salvation, or exaltation, is solely dependent upon the works of men. In the words of Mormon Apostle James Talmage:

> Salvation is, and must be, a cooperative enterprise between God and man. (*An Understandable Religion*, p. 24)

Probably one of the most offensive tenets of Mormonism is their insistence that they are the only true Christian church on the face of the earth and that every other church is in a state of apostasy. The Mormons deny almost every fundamental of the Christian faith, and insist they alone represent true Christianity.

In 1973, Mormon Apostle Mark E. Peterson succinctly stated this Mormon position when he said:

> When the Savior established his church during his mortal ministry . . . one important fact became conspicuously clear: Salvation comes through the Church. It does not come through any separate organization or splinter group nor to any private party as an individual. . . . Therefore it was made clearly manifest that salvation is in the Church, and of the Church, and is obtained only through the Church. (*The Ensign*, July 1973, p. 108)

From the context it is clear that Peterson refers to the Church of Jesus Christ of Latter-day Saints as "the Church."

On October 6, 1990, an Associated Press article appeared in the *San Diego Union* entitled, "Mormons Warming to More Dialogue With Other Religious Groups." The article stated that while Mormons have generally kept aloof from other religious groups, they are now becoming more involved with them. The article also mentioned the mistrust Christians have toward the Mormon church.

That mistrust is justified when you discover that there is no way for Mormons to fellowship with Bible-believing Christians on equal terms since they believe themselves to be the only true church. This is a fundamental conviction of Mormonism that cannot be denied without denouncing the *Book of Mormon* itself.

We read in 1 Nephi 14:10:

> Behold there are save two churches only; the one is the church
> of the Lamb of God, and the other is the church of the devil; where-
> fore, whoso belongeth not to the church of the Lamb of God belong-
> eth to that great church, which is the mother of abominations; and
> she is the whore of all the earth.

Because the Mormons feel this exclusivity, they naturally feel com-
pelled to convert as many as possible to their way of thinking. The
"warming up" to other churches mentioned in the newspaper article
will help them accomplish that goal. The statistics seem to prove it,
because many converts to Mormonism once attended a Christian
church of one denomination or another.

2

Doesn't the persecution of the LDS church prove it is the true church?

Webster defines persecution as follows: "To afflict or harass constantly so as to injure or distress; oppress cruelly." Questioning the
beliefs of the Mormon church can hardly fit into the category of persecution.

Mormons are quick to point to Matthew 5:11 as a picture of the
persecution they receive. Matthew records Jesus as saying, "Blessed
are ye, when men shall revile you, and persecute you, and shall say all
manner of evil against you falsely, for my sake."

But Christ did not say persecution would be the only tell-tale sign
of true Christianity. In addition to Bible-believing Christians, a number of religious groups have faced harsh persecution.

Many Mormons, however, feel that questioning or criticizing their
doctrine is persecution. These people don't understand that their own
church leaders invited the criticism. In May of 1873, Brigham Young
preached:

I say to the whole world, receive the truth, no matter who presents it to you. Take up the Bible, compare the religion of the Latter-day Saints with it, and see if it will stand the test. (*Journal of Discourses*, 16:46)

Concerning the *Book of Mormon*, Apostle Orson Pratt said:

If after a rigid examination it be found an imposition, it should be extensively published to the world as such . . . not by physical force, neither by persecutions, bare assertions nor ridicule, but by strong and powerful arguments by evidences adduced from Scripture and reason. . . . (*Divine Authenticity of the Book of Mormon*, pp. 1–2)

Claims concerning the *Book of Mormon*, and many of the doctrines of Mormonism, cannot stand the test Brigham Young and Orson Pratt described. Mormon doctrine does not compare with that found in the Bible. To expose those flaws can hardly be called persecution.

My motive in studying Mormonism is concern for the Mormon, not antagonism. Brigham Young endorsed the freedom to express differences in a message on June 19, 1859:

If I should hear a man advocate the erroneous principles he had imbibed through education, and oppose those principles, some might imagine that I was opposed to that man, when in fact I am only opposed to every evil and erroneous principle he advances. (*Journal of Discourses*, 7:191)

If Brigham Young can make a statement like that, it is only fair that others be given the same courtesy. My argument is not with the Mormon in particular, but with what I feel are the erroneous principles of Mormonism.

| 3 |

Which church is the true Church if it is not the LDS church?

The Mormon fails to realize that when Christ said He was coming for a church without spot or wrinkle (Ephesians 5:27), He in no way implied He was coming for a church *building* or some *legal organization* recognized by the government as a church.

It is entirely possible to be a member of an organized religion and not be a member of Christ's Church. Membership in the true Church comes only by being born anew into it, by accepting Jesus Christ as your personal Savior and allowing Him to bring about the necessary rebirth.

The true Church is made up of individuals, not four walls. It might surprise some, but as far as God is concerned, there are no Mormons, Muslims, Buddhists, Baptists, Presbyterians, Methodists, Pentecostals, Lutherans, or even atheists. He sees only saved Christians or lost sinners.

The claim of any church organization to be the one true church is proof to anyone who knows the Scriptures that it is, in fact, a false church. *No* church organization has the authority or power to save; that comes only through Jesus Christ and Him alone. "Neither is there salvation in any other: for there is none other name under heaven given among men, whereby we must be saved" (Acts 4:12).

The Bible refers to the true Church as the *Body of Christ*. In 1 Corinthians 12:27, the apostle Paul says that as a believer, ". . . ye are the body of Christ, and members in particular." This is the Church Jesus Christ is coming for, not charlatans who give people a false hope by telling them that membership in their organization will take care of everything. You can attend church services five times a week, give double tithes, be baptized, or even teach a Sunday school class, and still be just as much on your way to hell as a person who doesn't recognize God at all.

The true Church is made up of people who have acknowledged the fact that they are sinners in need of forgiveness. "For all have sinned, and come short of the glory of God" (Romans 3:23).

The Church is also made up of those who realize that there is absolutely nothing they can do to buy their salvation and have put their total trust in Jesus Christ. The Bible says we cannot trust ourselves:

"Who can say, I have made my heart clean, I am pure from my sin?" (Proverbs 20:9).

"For by grace are ye saved through faith; and that not of yourselves: it is the gift of God: Not of works, lest any man should boast" (Ephesians 2:8–9).

Those who have discovered these truths and embraced them are part of the true Church.

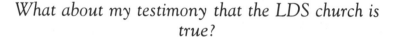

4

What about my testimony that the LDS church is true?

One of the biggest deceptions that the Mormon church puts over men and women is to have them pray to determine whether or not the message contained in the *Book of Mormon* is true. In fact, the *Book of Mormon* does not contain much of the doctrine peculiar to the Mormon faith. If Mormons really read it closely, they would find many points that, in fact, contradict Mormon theology.

No doubt, the Mormon hierarchy is aware that a great majority of the people in this country have had some upbringing in the Bible. Though verses of Scripture may never have been memorized, the main concept of who God is, the coming of Jesus Christ to earth, and of the message He brought forth are still in the back of the person's mind.

In giving the prospective convert the *Book of Mormon* to read, the LDS church knows he will read things that are quite familiar to him. Instead of receiving the testimony that the doctrines of Mormonism are true, he will in reality be reading doctrine he has learned from the Bible, possibly years ago. Unknowingly, he will relate the Mormon church with the doctrines he has come to know, and accept the Mormon church as true without even realizing it does not accept many things written in the *Book of Mormon* and the Bible.

For example, the *Book of Mormon* declares that God is a spirit (Alma 18:24–28), while Mormonism insists God has a body of flesh and bones (*Doctrine and Covenants*, sec. 130:22).

The *Book of Mormon* teaches there is only one God (2 Nephi 31:21), while Mormonism teaches there are many Gods (*Teachings of the Prophet Joseph Smith*, p. 370).

If the Mormon church is as honest as it claims to be (see Article 13 in *Articles of Faith*), it should perhaps instruct potential converts to read *Doctrine and Covenants* or *The Book of Abraham*, for in these books we find Mormon doctrine in its purer form.

Scripturally, the practice of praying about truth is not biblical. The apostle John warns us:

> . . . believe not every spirit, but try the spirits whether they are of God: because many false prophets are gone out into the world (1 John 4:1).

The word for *try* used by the apostle is the Greek word *dokimazo*, which means literally "to test, examine, or prove." We are to test or examine what we hear with the standard for truth: the Bible.

Praying over the *Book of Mormon* makes about as much sense as praying whether or not it is all right to steal. We know stealing is wrong because the Bible clearly says it is wrong. Likewise, praying over religious books such as the *Book of Mormon* is wrong.

I am not saying we should not be in prayer during a testing process, but I am saying prayer is not to be *the* test. Pray rather for guidance as to *what* to look for and *where* to look concerning what is being said. If your conclusions show contradictions between what is said and what the Bible says, be assured it is not the Bible that is wrong.

There are millions of lost souls within religions around the world who will testify that their belief is true because they prayed and felt it was right. Sincerity, however, does not determine truth. "There is a way which seemeth right unto a man, but the end thereof are the ways of death" (Proverbs 14:12).

5

If the Mormon church is wrong, why is it the fastest growing church today?

Bear in mind that the earth's entire population was outside the Ark during the Great Flood. Does this mean the world was right and Noah wrong? Though the population of true believers far exceeds the number of Mormons, Christians are still a minority compared to the rest of the world's religions. If numbers of adherents determined truth, then the Roman Catholic Church and Islam rank at the top.

The rapid rise of organizations such as the Mormons, Moonies, Jehovah's Witnesses, etc., does not in any way reflect upon the truthfulness of their doctrines, but instead proves just how true the words of the Savior were when He said:

> And many false prophets shall rise, and shall deceive many. (Matthew 24:11)

The apostle Peter also confirmed this in his epistle:

> But there were false prophets also among the people, even as there shall be false teachers among you, who privily shall bring in damnable heresies, even denying the Lord that brought them, and bring upon themselves swift destruction. And many shall follow their pernicious ways; by reason of whom the way of truth shall be evil spoken of. (2 Peter 2:1–2)

6

Didn't Jesus say His true Church would have His name in it?

Mormons contend that because Christian denominations have many different names which do not specifically contain the Lord's name, they cannot be God's true Church. When this issue is brought up, the Mormon will proudly point out that the name of his church meets this "qualification."

The fact is little known, even to many Latter-day Saints, that their church was not always known as "The Church of Jesus Christ of Latter-day Saints." When founded, it was simply called "The Church of Christ." According to one of the three witnesses to the *Book of Mormon*, David Whitmer, this was the name given by the Lord. (*An Address to All Believers in Christ*, p. 73)

Despite what Whitmer says about the name being given by the Lord, we find that the church voted to change the name to "The Church of the Latter-day Saints" in 1834 (*History of the Church*, 2:63). Notice the Lord's name was completely absent.

In 1838 Joseph Smith had a revelation about the name of the church, and it was changed to "The Church of Jesus Christ of Latter-day Saints," as it stands today.

Mormon Apostle Bruce McConkie emphasizes the use of Jesus' name in the church's name:

> The resurrected Christ gave to the Nephites this test whereby they might distinguish the true church from any other: 1. It would be called in his name, for "how be it my church save it be called in my name?" (Bruce McConkie, *Mormon Doctrine*, p.139)

McConkie draws his conclusion from 3 Nephi 27:8, which says:

> And how shall it be my church save it be called in my name? For if a church be called in Moses' name then it be Moses' church; or if it be called in the name of a man then it be the church of man. . . .

This argument has many weaknesses. Nowhere in the entire Bible do we find true believers belonging to any "church" with the name of Christ on it. Instead, we find that the "called out ones," which is what the Greek word for "church," *ekklesia*, literally means, were identified rather by their geographical location.

The apostle Paul identifies the believers in Corinth as "the church of God, which is at Corinth." To those in Galatia, he addressed his letter to the "the churches of Galatia." In both the first and second letter to the Thessalonians, he refers to the Christians as belonging to "the church of the Thessalonians."

By the reasoning of 3 Nephi 27:8, Paul must have been writing to a false church. This, of course, is absurd.

God recognizes His people by their faith in Him, not by a name written over the door.

7

Doesn't the fact that there are so many Christian denominations prove Christianity can't be true?

A common misunderstanding among Mormons and many non-Christians is that because there are many Christian denominations, they must all disagree with each other, believing their individual denomination is the only true sect. The outsider might expect a sort of spiritual "free-for-all." This, of course, is not the case.

Though various denominations may disagree on certain points, most differences are minor and will in no way prohibit anyone from being truly saved. For example, the fact that one believes the rapture of the Church will take place before the tribulation, while another believes it will take place during or after it, has nothing to do with the core doctrine of salvation.

Some think the two witnesses described in the book of Revelation are Elijah and Moses, while others disagree. But no matter who they are, it will not cost a person his gift of eternal life if the wrong choice is made concerning these matters.

What is important and vital to salvation is what an individual believes and acts upon concerning the Bible's basic truths of salvation and who God is. If the mark is missed on these, it is missed completely.

Basically, all Christian denominations hold to these biblical truths:

- The Bible is the infallible Word of God and the only authority concerning spiritual matters.
- There is one God revealed through three personages—the Father, the Son, and the Holy Spirit.
- Jesus was truly God and truly man, and He came to earth to die and provide salvation for all who believe on Him.

Brigham Young

Following a brief power struggle after the death of Joseph Smith, Brigham Young led his followers to the Salt Lake Valley in 1847. No doubt Young is responsible for some of the more bizarre doctrines of Mormonism. On January 2, 1870, Young told his people, "I have never yet preached a sermon and sent it out to the children of men, that they may not call scripture" (Journal of Discourses, 13:95).

• Christ's birth (being born of a virgin) was indeed a miracle.
• Jesus rose again bodily from the dead.
• Salvation is a free gift and cannot be earned by doing good works.

Mormons give the impression that they are the only true church because they all believe the same things. What they don't tell you is that there are approximately a hundred different factions of Latter-day Saints who accept Joseph Smith as a prophet of God and the *Book of Mormon* as the word of God. Many of these splinter groups believe they alone are the true church that Joseph Smith was to restore. They likewise believe the other LDS churches are in a state of apostasy along with the various Christian denominations.

One of these splinter groups is the Reorganized Church of Jesus Christ of Latter-day Saints, headquartered in Independence, Missouri. It is the largest Mormon group outside of Salt Lake City, Utah, though they do not like to be referred to as "Mormons." They followed Joseph Smith's son as their second president and prophet rather than accept Brigham Young as the successor to the "martyred prophet." Traditionally, they have always had presidents who were descendants of Joseph Smith. Other splinter groups include the Strangites, the Cutlerites, the Temple Lot Mormons, the Church of the Lamb of God, the Church of Christ, the Church of Jesus Christ of the Children of Zion, Christ's Church of the First Born, the Church of the Messiah, and the Church of Jesus Christ of Israel—to name a few.

Even if the accusation that the various Christian denominations fight among themselves were true, the argument for a unified LDS church is still weak. Latter-day Saints are splintered and at odds over several issues critical to the unity of the Latter-day Saint movement.

8

Why don't Christian churches have apostles and prophets as the foundation of their Church as the Mormon church has?

Mormonism stands or falls on its foundation of prophetic and apostolic leaders.

"Several characteristics are peculiar to our faith. Among them is its organization with prophets and apostles, who Paul said are the foundation of the Church" (Elder James E. Faust of the Quorum of the Twelve Apostles, *Ensign*, May, 1980, p. 12).

The Mormons use Ephesians 2:20 as their scriptural support for this belief. It reads:

And are built upon the foundation of the apostles and prophets, Jesus Christ himself being the chief corner stone.

The problem appears to be that Mormons are only reading half the verse. They fail to recognize the importance of the words: "Jesus Christ himself being the chief corner stone."

Webster describes a cornerstone as a foundation. We must ask ourselves: "What is the foundation of the apostles and prophets?" The answer is *Jesus Christ.* He is the foundation and/or chief cornerstone. We know this to be true because the Bible reminds us of the fact in 1 Corinthians 3:11:

For other foundation can no man lay than that is laid, which is *Jesus Christ* (italics added).

Does it seem logical that Paul would contradict himself by saying the foundation of the church is the organization of apostles and prophets and then say the only foundation of the true church is Jesus Christ? There is no other foundation than Jesus Christ.

Not only do Mormons wrongly insist they are the only true church because they have prophets and apostles, but they must answer why they have reversed the order of the offices. In the LDS church government, the *prophet* sits at the top, over the apostles. But the Bible specifically says in 1 Corinthians 12:28:

> And God hath set some in the church, *first apostles, secondarily prophets.* . . . (italics added).

The New Testament order of authority clearly differs from that of the Old Testament. But the Mormon office of prophet reflects the order of the Old Testament. In fact, Mormons use the verse in Amos 3:7 to support their beliefs:

> Surely the Lord will do nothing but He revealeth his secret unto His servants the prophets.

The Office of a Prophet

The New Testament has this to say about the old prophetical order:

> For all the prophets and the law prophesied until John. (Matthew 11:13)
> The law and the prophets were until John. . . . (Luke 16:16)

The appearance of John the Baptist marked the end of the Old Testament era. Though he was the last of the prophets to proclaim the coming of the Messiah, his sudden execution by King Herod prevented him from seeing the New Testament era unfold.

Before the completion of God's written revelation, Old Testament prophets transmitted messages from God to the people. They were the spokesmen for the Almighty (much as the Mormon prophet claims to be). In the New Testament the situation is quite different.

Hebrews 1:1–2 reveals this:

> God, who at sundry times and in divers manners spake in times past unto the fathers by the prophets, hath in these last days spoken unto us by His Son. . . .

The Office of the Son

The Old Testament message was fully realized in Jesus Christ, God manifest in the flesh. While the Old Testament prophesied His coming, the New Testament declares His arrival. And with His coming came the preaching of the Good News of the Gospel of the Kingdom of God.

Christians are *followers of Christ*. The Greek word "Christian" actually means "little Christs." As believers, we seek to live a life which emulates that of our Savior. We take Jesus at His word, declaring Him to be trustworthy. During His ministry on earth He validated the Old Testament scriptures by constantly quoting from them. Faithful followers recorded His words as future reference for how Christians should live and believe.

When the time came for the Messiah to leave His small flock, He commissioned His disciples to spread the message of salvation and to strengthen God's church. Thus, as Christians, we must find our guidance not only in the Old Testament, but also in the New Testament Epistles, written by His chosen disciples—inspired by the Holy Spirit, and of course in the words of our Lord himself, which are also recorded there.

Jesus did not leave His church to wander about without direction, but left us God's revealed Word: the Bible. It is the handbook of the true Christian. The Bible, and the Bible alone, is our standard of truth. By it all things must be judged.

If a person claims to have a message from God, it must be in complete harmony with the Scriptures. God has no lapse of memory; He will not contradict what He has said earlier.

The Lord still speaks to His people through the Holy Spirit, but often people claim the Spirit has told them things that contradict what God has already said. This cannot be.

The best test of whether or not the Holy Spirit is speaking is to compare the message with the Scriptures. If anyone thinks the Lord has told him something that contradicts His Word, we can be certain it was not the Lord speaking.

The Office of an Apostle

What is an apostle? The word comes from the Greek *apostolos*, meaning "one sent forth." While it is true that our Lord chose twelve men to be "apostles," we learn from the Bible that this number was not to be regarded as a standard. Throughout the New Testament many others are referred to as apostles who were not part of the original twelve. For example, Barnabas is called an apostle in Acts 14:14. And in Romans 16:7 Paul lists Andronicus and Junia as apostles. We know that James, the son of Zebedee, and James, the son of Alpheus were chosen as part of the twelve, but Paul also names James, the Lord's brother, as an apostle in Galatians 1:19. Many men sent forth to preach the Good News were called apostles.

Mormons insist there should be an exact number of twelve ordained apostles (except in the case of a vacancy caused by death). But even in this point, the LDS church cannot claim consistency.

According to the *Book of Mormon*, Jesus, when He supposedly came in the flesh to this continent, ordained twelve men to be His disciples. This was done while there were still twelve apostles in Palestine. Twelve here and twelve there make twenty-four apostles—hardly an authoritative quorum according to the Mormons' claim.

But we cannot stop at twenty-four either. The preface of 3 Nephi 28 states that three of these twelve were to "remain alive on earth until the Lord comes." We read in 3 Nephi 28:7–8:

> Therefore, more blessed are ye, for ye shall never taste of death; but ye shall live to behold all the doings of the Father unto the children of men, even until all things shall be fulfilled according to the will of the Father, when I shall come in my glory with the powers of heaven. And ye shall never endure the pains of death; but when I shall come in my glory ye shall be changed in the twinkling of an eye from mortality to immortality; and then shall ye be blessed in the kingdom of my Father.

Doctrine and Covenants, section seven, says the apostle John is still alive somewhere on the earth. The preface to this section claims this revelation is the "translated version of the record made on parchment by John and hidden up by himself." Verses 1–3 easily demonstrate how Joseph Smith twisted the words of John 21:22–23. Joseph Smith's version reads:

> And the Lord said unto me: John, my beloved, what desirest thou? For if you shall ask what you will, it shall be granted unto you.

And I said unto him: Lord, give unto me power over death, that I may live and bring souls unto thee.

And the Lord said unto me: Verily, verily, I say unto thee, because thou desirest this thou shalt tarry until I come in my glory, and shalt prophesy before nations, kindreds, tongues, and people.

To sum things up, the twelve apostles of the LDS church today, the three Nephites in the *Book of Mormon*, and the apostle John, total sixteen apostles! Even if we excluded the three Nephites and John, why hasn't the Mormon church ordained twelve more apostles for the Eastern Hemisphere just as Jesus supposedly did for the Western in the *Book of Mormon*?

Conclusion of the Matter

A prophet is one who "speaks the things of God," and cannot be thought of as one who only predicts future events. Surely the Mormon church would not limit their prophet to merely the roll of seer, since no LDS prophet of recent years has made any attempt at predicting the future. By the very definition of the word "prophet," we must conclude that the Christian Church still has functioning prophets today, though not in the same sense as Mormons see it.

Mormons insist that only one man can be a prophet at any given time, and that this prophet is necessary to guide their church. The Bible, however, says the task of guidance is given to the Holy Spirit. John 16:13 states:

Howbeit when he, the Spirit of truth, is come, he will guide you into all truth. . . .

The Lord has raised up many men of God whom other Christians emulate and follow. Some of these great men have been considered "prophets" of their day by fellow believers. But whatever their title, they, like all believers, are subject to the Scriptures and must come under its authority.

Mormon leaders in the past have proclaimed they are not under biblical authority, or any written authority for that matter. In 1980 Ezra Taft Benson, who at that time was an apostle (later becoming Mormonism's thirteenth president in 1985), delivered a speech entitled "Fourteen Fundamentals in Following the Prophets." In this speech he declared the living Mormon prophet to be a more vital authority to the Mormon church than their standard works (the Bible, the *Book of Mormon, Doctrine and Covenants*, and *Pearl of Great Price*).

To illustrate his position, Benson proceeded to tell how Brigham Young took copies of the Bible, the *Book of Mormon*, and *Doctrine and Covenants*, and after laying them down in front of him, said,

> There is the written word of God to us, concerning the work of God from the beginning of the world to our day. When compared with the living oracles those books are nothing to me; those books do not convey the word of God direct to us now, as do the words of a Prophet or a man bearing the Holy Priesthood in our day and generation. I would rather have the living oracles than all the writing in the books.

Benson went on to relate how Joseph Smith (who was present), said,

> Brother Brigham has told you the word of the Lord, and he has told you the truth.

What we really have here is a violation of Jeremiah 17:5:

> Thus saith the Lord; Cursed be the man that trusteth in man, and maketh flesh his arm, and whose heart departeth from the Lord.

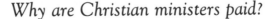

9

Why are Christian ministers paid?

The subject of a paid clergy has been the topic of controversy since the time of Paul. Because many Christian pastors receive compensation for their services to churches, Mormons accuse them of being "hirelings." They often boast about their unpaid elders, that they are not in the ministry for "filthy lucre."

Before the Mormons drastically revamped their temple ceremony in

1990, Christian pastors were portrayed as being on Satan's payroll. Lucifer approached a Christian pastor and said to him, "If you will preach your orthodox religion to these people and convert them, I will pay you well."

Since this "orthodox religion" is considered by Mormons to be laden with false doctrine, Christian leaders are assumed to be teaching false doctrine for monetary gain.

This argument is hardly new, as we see in Paul's letter to the Corinthian church. Throughout 1 Corinthians 9, Paul defends the idea of paid ministers while explaining why he chose not to receive compensation. He defends his position by stating he had never used his position to take an offering from the Corinthians lest they accuse him of being in the ministry for the money. The context reveals Paul's reason for this as the immaturity and selfishness of the Corinthian believers. At no time does the epistle imply that a paid ministry is unbiblical.

It is common knowledge that Paul did have an occupation as a tentmaker (Acts 18:3); however, he never says it was wrong for a minister to receive a salary for his labors in the Lord's work. In fact, he strongly supports the idea of a paid ministry.

In 1 Corinthians 9:4–5, he establishes the fact that ministers are like any human being. They must eat, support their families, and pay their bills. He uses the example of the soldier, who never goes to war at his own expense (v. 7). He further states that a farmer eats the fruit of what he has planted and a shepherd drinks the milk of his flock. In light of these examples he asks in verse 11 if it is wrong for the pastor, who feeds his flock spiritually, to partake of their carnal (material) things; after all, the pastor spends his day serving his people just as the farmer serves his customers by selling his fruits.

Paul further reminds the Corinthians in verse 13 that the priests in the Temple lived by the things of the Temple. The priest's entire job was ministering to the people (Numbers 18:1–7). To guarantee priestly service, the tribe of Levi was not granted an inheritance in the Promised Land as the other tribes were. Instead, a tithe (tenth) was gathered from all the children of Israel to sustain the Levites:

> And, behold, I have given the children of Levi all the tenth in Israel for an inheritance, for their service which they serve, even the service of the tabernacle of the congregation. (Numbers 18:21)

Paul insists that the Lord has consecrated those who have devoted their entire lives to ministering to the spiritual needs of their flock, and therefore should be supported by that flock:

> Even so hath the Lord ordained that they which preach the gospel should live of the gospel. (1 Corinthians 9:14)

We know that Paul accepted love offerings from other Christians, for he says so in 2 Corinthians 11:8:

> I robbed other churches, taking wages of them, to do you service.

Knowing this was a touchy subject with the Corinthians, he chose not to receive money from them. Our Lord also supported the concept of a paid ministry when He stated in Luke 10:7 that the laborer is worthy of his hire.

Mormon missionaries have often boasted about how they are not paid while on their mission. In some cases the missionary himself has saved for his mission, but this is not always the case. Funds given to support the missionaries on their mission are sent to the LDS church in return for a tax deductible receipt. The church in turn sends the funds to the missionary. On November 27, 1990, the *Salt Lake Tribune* announced that the Mormon church, beginning January 1, 1991, would contribute $350 monthly to missionaries called from the United States or Canada, no matter where they are assigned. This was to alleviate the financial burden missionary service places on families and individuals. Clearly this is a paid ministry.

Although the bishop of the local Mormon ward is not paid, the *Doctrine and Covenants* says he should be! Section 42:73 says:

> And the bishop, also, shall receive his support, or a just remuneration for all his services in the church.

There are many workers in the Mormon church who receive salaries for their labors. The church employs many secretaries, bookkeepers, lawyers, public relations people, seminary professors, institute teachers, and gardeners—all of whom receive paychecks from the church.

The general authorities of the LDS church also receive compensation for their position in the church. Though these salaries are hardly exorbitant, they are quite large compared to the salary the public is made to believe they receive.

Since it is quite profitable in Utah for large businesses to have LDS general authorities on their board, many companies ask them to serve as paid board members.

To state that the Mormon church has an unpaid ministry is very misleading. On the other hand, the Bible does not condemn the support of ministers. In fact, we find that both the Old and New Testaments declare it perfectly acceptable.

10

Wasn't there a total apostasy of the Church?

To say there was a total apostasy would be to credit Jesus Christ with a gross lie.

When Peter declared the eternal truth that Jesus was "the Christ, the Son of the Living God" (Matthew 16:16), our Lord responded by saying:

> Upon this rock will I build my church; and the gates of hell shall not prevail against it. (Matthew 16:18)

Despite Jesus' clear indication that the gates of hell would never prevail against Christ's Church, Mormon Apostle Orson Pratt, on April 10, 1870, stated:

> Jesus made his appearance on the earth in the meridian of time, and he established his kingdom on the earth . . . the kingdoms of this world made war against the kingdom of God, established eighteen centuries ago, and they prevailed against it, and the kingdom ceased to exist. (*Journal of Discourses*, 13:125)

Mormonism teaches that this "rock" upon which the Church is built is "the rock of revelation," even though the Bible plainly declares the rock to be none other than Jesus Christ. The Church would be founded upon Jesus Christ! Acts 4:11–12 verifies this:

> This is the stone which was set at nought of you builders, which is become the head of the corner. Neither is there salvation in any

other: for there is none other name under heaven given among men, whereby we must be saved.

The name whereby we must be saved is Jesus Christ—not the Church of Jesus Christ of Latter-day Saints, or Joseph Smith—but Jesus Christ!

The Mormon church uses 1 Timothy 4:1 to substantiate its claim that there was a total apostasy, and prove the need for a restoration—namely the Mormon church. But Paul tells us that only some would depart, not all:

> Now the Spirit speaketh expressly, that in the latter times some shall depart from the faith, giving heed to seducing spirits, and doctrines of devils.

Ephesians 5:25–32 illustrates Christ's concern for the welfare of His church. When speaking on the subject of husbands and wives, Paul uses the comparison of Christ and the church:

> Husbands, love your wives, even as Christ also loved the church, and gave himself for it. That he might sanctify and cleanse it with the washing of water by the word, that he might present it to himself a glorious church, not having spot, or wrinkle, or any such thing; but that it should be holy and without blemish. So ought men to love their wives as their own bodies. He that loveth his wife, loveth himself. For no man ever yet hated his own flesh; but nourisheth and cherisheth it, even as the Lord the church . . . This is a great mystery; but I speak concerning Christ and the church.

Just as it is wrong to neglect the welfare of our wives, so would it be if Christ were to neglect the welfare of His church. Accusing Him of letting His church fall into a total apostasy would be blasphemous. As a man nourishes himself, so would Christ nourish His church.

God has always had a people. Even in the Old Testament when it seemed all of Israel had failed God and turned to idol worship, there was always a remnant, somewhere, who refused to lower themselves by serving any other god but the one, true God. Even when the prophet Elijah thought he was the only one who still had faith in the true and living God, God showed him that He still had 7,000 men who had not bowed the knee to Baal! (1 Kings 19:18).

The claim of a total apostasy not only contradicts the message in the Bible, but also contradicts the *Book of Mormon*. Third Nephi 28:1–8 tells us that Jesus Christ supposedly told three Nephite disciples that they would never taste of death but remain alive until the Lord's coming in the clouds. Three of Christ's own disciples were actually to remain alive on this earth until the second coming. Did they apostatize also? A *total* apostasy would mean that they had.

Jesus said:

> For where two or three are gathered in my name, there am I in the midst of them. (Matthew 18:20)

The introduction to the *History of the Church*, page XL, states that without total apostasy, there would have been no need for the Mormon church.

> Nothing less than a complete apostasy of the Christian religion would warrant the establishment of the Church of Jesus Christ of Latter-day Saints.

If the account of the three witnesses in the *Book of Mormon* were true, there is no reason for the Mormon church to exist.

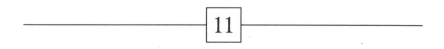

11

Where do you get your authority?

Unlike the Mormon, who claims his authority in a human priesthood, the true believer's authority comes from the living Word of God, the Bible:

> But as many as received him, to them gave he power [authority] to become the sons of God, even to them that believe on his name. (John 1:12)

If you have accepted Christ as your Savior, you have been given the power, authority, or right, to be a son of God! Your faith in Jesus Christ has given you this authority, and no man can change that fact by a new set of rules. Romans 8:14–17 exemplifies that authority:

For as many as are led by the Spirit of God, they are the sons of God. For ye have not received the spirit of bondage again to fear; but ye have received the Spirit of adoption, whereby we cry, Abba, Father. The Spirit itself beareth witness with our spirit, that we are the children of God: And if children, then heirs; heirs of God, and joint-heirs with Christ; if so be that we suffer with him, that we may be also glorified together.

If Jesus Christ says we have this authority through believing in Him, then we have it! Any person or church organization that claims an authority other than this does so against the decree of God.

Mormons claim their authority comes from the Aaronic and Melchizedek priesthoods. What they fail to realize is they do not have any right to hold either priesthood.

The Aaronic Priesthood

The spiritual significance of the Aaronic, or Levitical, offices ended with the death of Christ (John 19:30). The term "priest" (Hebrew, *cohen*), means "one who stands up for another and mediates his cause." Before the Great Sacrifice, the priest had to stand in the gap for the people and offer animal sacrifices to atone for their sins. Mormons, who claim to hold the Aaronic priesthood, have nothing to do with sacrifice. Therefore, their office is not really a restoration of the original, as we are led to believe.

One would think a church that spends so much time in genealogical work would know better than to claim the Levitical priesthood. That priesthood was reserved *only* for Aaron and his descendants:

And thou shalt appoint Aaron and his sons, and they shall wait on their priest's office: and the stranger that cometh nigh shall be put to death. (Numbers 3:10–11)

Even the *Doctrine and Covenants* denies this office to those not related to Aaron:

No man has a legal right to this office, to hold the keys to this [Aaronic] priesthood except he be a literal descendant of Aaron. (*Doctrine and Covenants*, 107:16)

The rule was so stringent, not even Christ could hold this priesthood, for He was of the tribe of Judah:

> For it is evident that our Lord sprang out of Judah; of which tribe Moses spake nothing concerning priesthood. (Hebrews 7:14)

The Melchizedek Priesthood

The Mormons also claim the Melchizedek priesthood, an office they have no right to hold. Outside of Melchizedek himself and Jesus Christ, there is no mention of anyone connected with the Melchizedek order.

Hebrews 7:21, speaking of Christ, declares:

> Thou art a priest for ever after the order of Melchizedek.

What is this order?

> First being by interpretation King of righteousness, and after that also King of Salem, which is, King of peace; without father, without mother, without descent, having neither beginning of days, nor end of life; but made like unto the Son of God; abideth a priest continually. (Hebrews 7:2–3)

Christ met every one of these qualifications. He is Righteousness (1 John 3:7) and He is Peace (Ephesians 2:14). Since Christ is God, He has neither father nor mother, nor beginning of days, nor end of life, and He was made like unto the Son of God (John 1:14).

Restoration of the Priesthood

Mormons place a strong emphasis on priesthood. They believe the Aaronic priesthood was restored to earth by John the Baptist when he appeared to Joseph Smith and Oliver Cowdery on the bank of the Susquehanna River on May 15, 1829.

Mormons view the Melchizedek priesthood as the greater of the two offices. If a Mormon is aspiring to become a god and rule his own kingdom throughout eternity, this office is a must. This priesthood gives him the necessary authority over the spiritual ordinances of his church. Since those outside the LDS church do not hold this office defined by modern-day revelation, Mormons feel the non-Mormon has no authority to administer Baptism, the Lord's Supper, or even the laying on of hands. In the words of Bruce McConkie:

> Without the Melchizedek Priesthood, salvation in the kingdom of God would not be available for men on earth, for the ordinances of salvation—the laying on of hands for the gift of the Holy Ghost, for instance—could not be authoritatively performed. Thus, as far as all religious organizations now existing are concerned, the presence or absence of this priesthood establishes the divinity or falsity of a professing church. (*Mormon Doctrine*, p. 479)

While most Mormon history is quite detailed, the issue of when the Melchizedek priesthood was reintroduced to this earth is still a mystery. The *History of the Church* assumes that the Melchizedek Priesthood was given to Joseph Smith sometime between May 15, 1829 and April 1830 (1:41). Other speculation places it between May 15 and June 1829. Whenever it happened, Smith claimed the priesthood was conferred upon him by Peter, James, and John.

Christ gives the true believer a royal priesthood (1 Peter 2:9). We are also living sacrifices (Romans 12:1), given fully to Christ, that we should offer praises unto Him who brought us out of darkness and into that marvelous light, which is Jesus Christ.

As holders of this royal priesthood, we are to stand and intercede for people, not to offer sacrifices for the cleansing of their sins, but to pray that they might turn to the one who cleanses from sin, namely Christ Jesus.

I have noticed increasingly in recent years how many Mormon authors, most of whom would quickly point to their "priesthood authority" in the Melchizedek priesthood, have been placing disclaimers in their books. Even Mormon General Authorities have prefaced their writings with the claim that their books are not official church publications and may not represent official LDS church policy. This would seem to tell us that the Mormon church, which claims sole authority when it comes to gospel matters, has within its ranks leaders who don't speak with full authority.

A Mormon may point to the prophet of his church as the true authority, but even his words can become null and void after he dies. Ezra Taft Benson made this clear in his "14 Fundamentals in Following the Prophet" speech. He stated that Mormons are not to pit dead prophets against living prophets, and that the words of the living prophet supersede those of the dead: "Beware of those who would pit the dead prophets, for the living prophets always take precedence" (Ezra Taft Benson, "14 Fundamentals," Press Copy, p. 5).

In reality, Mormons have no firm basis for truth other than the words of sinful man.

12

How can the Bible be God's inerrant Word and contain so many contradictions?

For many years, critics have said that the Bible is filled with gross contradictions, and therefore ought not to be trusted. However, if one looks closely at these so-called discrepancies, the difficulties are erased.

One of the difficulties most frequently brought up by Mormons is the passage in Acts 9:7. Here we find the story of the conversion of Saul while he was on his way to Damascus. The account says that the men who were with Saul heard the voice of Christ.

Later in Acts 22:9 we read that they did not hear a voice:

And they that were with me saw indeed the light, and were afraid; but they heard not the voice of him that spake to me.

Greek scholar W. F. Arndt explains it this way in his book *Does the Bible Contradict Itself?*:

The construction of the verb "to hear," *akouo*, is not the same in both accounts. In Acts 9:7 it is used in the genitive; in Acts 22:9 with the accusative. The construction with the genitive simply expresses that something is being heard or that certain sounds reach the ear; nothing indicates whether or not the person understands what he hears.

The construction with the accusative, however, describes a hearing which includes mental apprehension of the message spoken. From this it becomes evident that the two passages are not contradictory.

Acts 22:9 does not deny that the associates of Paul heard certain sounds; it simply declares that they did not hear in such a way as to understand what was being said. Our English idiom in this case is not so expressive as the Greek. (*Does the Bible Contradict Itself?*, pp. 13–14; used by permission)

The same difficulty over the use of "hear" can arise in English. Have you ever had someone call you from another room and you yelled back, "What? I didn't hear you." Obviously, you heard, but you didn't understand the message.

Mormons also bring up other verses in order to "prove" the Bible is full of errors. They often refer to Matthew 27:5 and Acts 1:18, which give accounts of the death of Judas. Matthew 27:5 claims that after Judas left the Temple, he went out and hanged himself. The account in Acts 1:18 says he fell headlong, burst open in the middle, and all his bowels gushed out.

But the only way this could be a contradiction is if Acts 1:18 said Judas did not hang himself, or if Matthew 27:5 said Judas did not fall headlong, etc. Who is to say that Judas did not hang himself, the rope broke, and his body fell, or that he fell on the way to hang himself? The writers are merely describing what *they* saw or heard—Matthew telling the story at the beginning, and Luke telling it as it no doubt appeared sometime later.

This explanation seems far more plausible than the wild tale invented by Mormon elder Heber C. Kimball, who said that the apostles killed Judas:

> Judas lost that saving principle, and they took him and killed him. It is said in the Bible that his bowels gushed out; but they actually kicked him until his bowels gushed out. (*Journal of Discourses*, 6:125–126)

The problem with most critics of the Bible is that they usually don't *want* to trust or believe its message, and therefore do not take the time to research apparent contradictions.

Mormons say they believe the Bible "as far as it is translated correctly." This is not a completely honest statement, because instead of turning to the Bible in the original languages to solve the problems of an incorrectly translated word, they prefer to give their personal interpretation.

As much as I love and admire the King James Version, I would never go so far as to say it is a perfect translation. There are many words that are poorly translated for today's English, even though they may have been excellent choices almost 400 years ago when the KJV was first introduced. The English language is a living language, changing constantly.

Genesis 1:28 illustrates the problems Mormons may encounter with the older language of the KJV. God told Adam and Eve to be fruitful and multiply and replenish the earth. "Replenish" means "fill again with what was there before." This implies that there was life on earth before Adam. Mormon Apostle, Orson Hyde, carried this further by giving a long description of the word "replenish" and concluded:

> The world was peopled before the days of Adam, as much so as it was before the days of Noah. (*Journal of Discourses*, 2:79)

However, the Hebrew word for "replenish," *millai*, in this passage means "fill." Many Bible versions use this better rendering. The New International Version reads: "Be fruitful and increase in number; fill the earth and subdue it."

When a Mormon resorts to attacking the Scriptures to defend his unbiblical positions, he has done nothing more than unbelievers have done throughout history. True followers of Jesus don't attack the Bible, they revere it as God's Word.* Our Lord said:

> Sanctify them through thy truth: thy word is truth. (John 17:17)

13

If the Bible is God's infallible Word, why are there so many versions?

To argue that the existence of various versions of the Bible is reason

---

*For further study on Bible difficulties, please see the following books: *Today's Handbook for Solving Bible Difficulties*, by David E. O'Brien (Bethany House Publishers), *Alleged Discrepancies of the Bible*, by John Haley (Baker Bookhouse), *Bible Difficulties & Seeming Contradictions*, by William F. Arndt (Concordia, 1987), and *The Encyclopedia of Bible Difficulties*, by Gleason L. Archer (Zondervan, 1982).

enough to mistrust all of them is just a smokescreen. Mormons mistrust the Bible because it is the book that refutes their doctrines.

You can take your pick of any version on the market today and you will find none of them support Mormonism—not even Joseph Smith's translation!

The Mormon church officially uses the King James Version of the Bible, used by God to bring countless people to a saving knowledge of His grace. A study of the history of this translation gives us every assurance of its reliability.

The Reliability of the Old Testament

The Old Testament text used in the King James translation was a wonder of accuracy when we consider the thousands of years between the original writings and their translation into English in 1611. Dr. E. F. Hills writes:

> After the Jews returned from the Babylonian exile, there was a great revival among the priesthood through the power of the Holy Spirit. "Not by might, nor by power, but by my Spirit, saith the Lord of hosts" (Zechariah 4:6). The Law was taught again in Jerusalem by Ezra, the priest who "had prepared his heart to seek the law of the Lord, and to do it, and to teach in Israel statutes and judgments" (Ezra 7:10). By Ezra and his successors, under the guidance of the Holy Spirit, all the Old Testament books were gathered together into one Old Testament canon, and their texts were purged of errors and preserved until the day of our Lord's earthly ministry. By that time the Old Testament text was so firmly established that even the Jews' rejection of Christ could not disturb it. Unbelieving Jewish scribes transmitted this traditional Hebrew Old Testament text, blindly but faithfully, until the dawn of the Protestant Reformation. As Augustine said long ago, these Jewish scribes were the librarians of the Christian Church. In the providence of God, they took care of the Hebrew Old Testament Scriptures until at length the time was ripe for Christians to make general use of them.
>
> According to G. F. Moore (1927), the earliest of these scribes are called Tannaim (teachers). These scribes not only copied the text of the Old Testament with great accuracy, but also committed to writing their oral tradition, called Mishna. These were followed by another group of scribes called Amoraim (Expositors). These were the

scholars who, in addition to their work as copyists of the Old Testament, also produced the Talmud, which is a commentary on the Mishna.

The Amoraim were followed in the sixth century by the Masoretes (Traditionalists) to whom the Masoretic (Traditional) Old Testament text is due. These Masoretes took extraordinary pains to transmit without error the Old Testament text which they had received from their predecessors. Many complicated safeguards against scribal slips were devised, such as counting the number of times each letter of the alphabet occurs in each book. Also critical material previously perpetrated only by oral instruction was put into writing. It is generally believed that the vowel points and other writing signs to aid in pronunciation were introduced into the text by the Masoretes.

It was the Traditional (Masoretic) text which was printed at the end of the medieval period. The first portion of the Hebrew Old Testament ever to issue from the press was the Psalms in 1477. In 1488 the entire Hebrew Bible was printed for the first time. A second edition was printed in 1491, and a third in 1494. This third edition was used by Luther in translating the Old Testament into German. Other faithful Protestant translations followed, including in due time the King James Version. Thus, it was that the Hebrew Old Testament text, divinely inspired and providentially preserved, was restored to the Church, to the circle of true believers. (*The King James Version Defended*, pp. 91–93; used by permission)

Dr. David Otis Fuller says, "Time has vindicated the original Hebrew text used in the King James Version. Recent archeological discoveries, such as the fragments of ancient texts found at the fortress Masada, prove the accuracy of the text. Parchment fragments at least 1900 years old containing portions of the Psalms, Leviticus, and Ezekiel were all virtually identical to the texts used for the KJV." (*Which Bible?*, pp. 8–10)

The Reliability of the New Testament

The story concerning the miraculous preservation of the Greek New Testament is also amazing.

Until about A.D. 300, the persecution of Christians was fierce. To take a stand for Christ meant putting your life on the line. This persecution diminished with the controversial conversion of the Roman emperor Constantine. From this time to the Reformation, Christianity became a status religion and became intermingled with many pagan accretions.

While Mormons might say Christianity ceased to exist, history does not bear this out. Just as God preserved a remnant who would not serve Baal in the Old Testament, He also saved a remnant during this dark period to preserve His Word. He used people such as the Waldensians to keep and preserve the true biblical text while much of organized Christianity of the time was busy corrupting theirs. The Waldensians stubbornly, under penalty of death, copied and recopied the biblical text, which later produced the *Textus Receptus*, or "received text." Luther used this text in his translation of the New Testament.

Joseph Smith's Translation

Joseph Smith's contempt for the Bible led him to write another one. The story behind the *Inspired Version*, or *Joseph Smith's Translation*, is quite interesting. We find in *Doctrine and Covenants* 73:4 that God supposedly told Joseph Smith to commence work on a new translation of the Bible and to finish it. In section 124:89 Smith is commanded to publish his new Bible. You would think that if God commanded such a thing, He would make a way for it to come to pass, especially since 1 Nephi 3:7 says:

> The Lord giveth no commandments unto the children of men, save he shall prepare a way for them that they may accomplish the thing which he commandeth them.

Despite this *Book of Mormon* promise, the tenth president of the Mormon church, Joseph Fielding Smith, insisted Joseph Smith's revision was not completed. He wrote:

> The reason that it has not been published by the Church is due to the fact that this revision was not completed . . . Due to persecution and mobbing this opportunity never came, so that the manuscript was left with only a partial revision. (*Answers to Gospel Questions*, 2:207)

What makes this statement so confusing is that the *History of the Church* quotes the Mormon founder as saying he did finish it:

> I [Joseph Smith] completed the translation of the New Testament, on the 2nd of February, 1833 and sealed it up, no more to be opened until it arrived in Zion. (1:324)

A footnote on the same page says the revision was to be published in Zion. Later in the same volume we find a letter written by Smith claiming he had finished his translation:

> We this day finished the translating of the Scriptures, for which we returned gratitude to our Heavenly Father. . . . (1:368)

This letter, addressed to "the Brethren in Zion," was signed by Sidney Rigdon, Joseph Smith, and F. G. Williams, and was dated July 2, 1833. These two dates in 1833 concur with those found in the *Church Chronology*, compiled by Mormon historian Andrew Jensen. He also writes that Smith finished the New Testament on February 2, 1833, and finished the entire Bible on July 2, 1833.

If Smith's Bible was indeed produced through divine inspiration, why didn't he consistently quote from it, and why did he sometimes contradict it in his sermons?

In his King Follett discourse delivered on April 6, 1844, Smith proclaimed to 20,000 listeners that Matthew 4:21 in the English New Testament was in error:

> I have an old edition of the New Testament in the Hebrew, Latin, German, and Greek languages. I have been reading the German, and find it to be the most correct translation, and to correspond nearest to the revelations which God has given to me for the last fourteen years. It tells about Jachoby, the son of Zebedee. It means Jacob . . . In the 21st verse of the fourth chapter of Matthew, my old German edition gives the word Jacob instead of James. (*Journal of Discourses*, 6:5)

Yet Smith's own version of Matthew 4:21 reads "James," not "Jacob."

A close examination of Smith's writings reveals that he ignored his own translation most of the time. Many of the Bible verses he altered in the *Book of Mormon* were not quoted the same in his revision. Smith went so far as to include a prophecy concerning his own birth in his version:

> And his name shall be called Joseph, and it shall be after the

name of his father; and he shall be like unto you; for the thing which the Lord shall bring forth by his hand shall bring my people salvation. (Genesis 50:33, JST*)

You would think that embarking on a new translation of the Bible would give Smith a perfect opportunity to clear up any apparent confusion on doctrine, yet we find that many of the scriptures which condemn Mormon doctrine were left intact by the prophet. This is probably because in 1833 Smith had not fully developed his erroneous viewpoints. What he left unchanged were portions he still may have believed to be true. Nonetheless, he did tamper with the Word of God and changed many portions to fit his unsound theology—without any support of the Hebrew or Greek text.

In spite of his translation, his theology changed. For example, while Mormonism teaches the existence of many gods, the JST tells us there is only one. In fact, the JST reads exactly as the KJV does when it says:

> Is there a God besides me? yea, there is no God; I know not any. (Isaiah 44:8, JST)

In fact, Mormon theologian Bruce McConkie acknowledges that the KJV Bible was the basis of Smith's work:

> While acting under the spirit of revelation, the Prophet corrected, revised, altered, added to, and deleted from the King James Version of the Bible. (*Mormon Doctrine*, p. 383)

But the evidence shows Smith did nothing more than attempt to pervert the Word of God.

Different translations of that Word are no threat to its credibility. Just as windows on a house allow us to view the inside from different perspectives, different Bible translations merely provide different perspectives on the same Truth. To say that the Bible is any less trustworthy because of the number of translations is nothing more than a Mormon smokescreen.

---

*Joseph Smith's Translation.

| 14 |

If the Bible is complete, what about all the books it mentions but does not include?

In order to gain the confidence of a skeptical world, Smith had to tear down faith in the only book that had the power to destroy his story in the *Book of Mormon*. To do this he inserted such phrases as:

> For behold, they have taken away from the gospel of the lamb many parts which are plain and most precious; and also many covenants of the Lord have they taken away. (1 Nephi 13:26)

Smith goes so far as to call everyone a fool who believes the Bible is the complete Word of God:

> Thou fool, that shall say: A Bible, we have got a Bible, and we need no more Bible. (2 Nephi 29:6)

Infused with such a low view of the Bible, Mormons love to call attention to lost books that they say should be in the Word of God. The Bible does mention writings that are not included in Scripture such as the Book of Nathan the Prophet, the Book of the War of the Lords, the Book of Jehu, and the Book of Enoch. *But* this does not mean that the Bible is incomplete.

In his book, *Articles of Faith*, James Talmage lists nearly 20 books mentioned in the Bible that he classifies as "missing scripture." (p. 502) In reality, the Mormon church does not believe these "missing scriptures" to be significant.

The *Doctrine and Covenants* says the *Book of Mormon* is the "fulness of the gospel" (20:9). It also states the *Book of Mormon* is the "fulness of the everlasting gospel" (27:5) and that the "fulness of the gospel" is found in the *Book of Mormon* (42:12). If the *Book of Mormon* were indeed the "gospel in its fullness," and if the missing books were really important, wouldn't they be contained in Smith's the *Book of Mormon*?

The Latter-day saint will try to tell you that the *Book of Mormon* is a translation of only a portion of the gold plates originally found by

Joseph Smith—that there are still more plates in God's safekeeping that have not been translated.

The *Doctrine and Covenants* refutes the claim that anything necessary has been left out:

> And I have sent forth the fulness of my gospel by the hand of Joseph Smith: and in weakness have I blessed him. (35:17)

The fullness of the gospel has already been sent forth and is found in the *Book of Mormon* according to this! Where is the Book of Jasher, the War of the Lords, the Book of Enoch? Surely if these books are as important as Mr. Talmage implies, the fullness of the gospel should contain them.

Furthermore, when Joseph Smith took it upon himself to retranslate the Bible, he also failed to include these books. Not one of them is mentioned any differently than the way they are mentioned in the King James Version. Not only did he not include the lost books, Smith lost another book. He left out the Song of Solomon in his *Inspired Version!*

15

Doesn't Genesis 1:26 prove there is more than one God and that He has a body of flesh and bones?

"And God said, Let us make man in our image, after our likeness: and let them have dominion over the fish of the sea, and over the fowl of the air, and over the cattle, and over all the earth, and over every creeping thing that creepeth upon the earth" (Genesis 1:26).

If this scripture proves anything, it proves the doctrine of the Trinity rather than the concept of three Gods. Mormons believe that because the scripture says, "let us make man," there is a plurality of Gods. Actually it means quite the opposite. The Hebrew word used for "God" here is *Elohim*. Elohim is the plural name for God. In verse 27 it reads, "God created man in His own image. . . ." If there were more than one God, it would have to read, "God made man in *their own* image. . . ." What we have is a plural noun used with a singular verb.

To further prove this point, turn to Deuteronomy 6:4: "Hear O Israel: The Lord our God is one Lord."

Mormonism teaches that God the Father is Elohim, and the Son is Jehovah. Yet literally translated, Deuteronomy 6:4 reads, "Hear O Israel: Jehovah our Elohim is one Jehovah." According to Mormon teaching, this is not possible, but the Bible's claim is clear.

One of the reasons Jewish people were so harshly persecuted was that they stubbornly insisted there was only one God. The Jews recognized the word Elohim to be a plural name. That is why Peter, on the day of Pentecost (Acts 2:38), stressed the fact that they must be baptized in the name of Jesus. The Jews recognized God the Father and the Holy Spirit, but in order to be saved they had to recognize the second person of the Trinity—Jesus Christ.

Mormons think that because this scripture says man was created in God's image, and we are flesh, God also must be flesh. Of course this is not the case. The Bible states many times that God is invisible (Hebrews 11:27; Colossians 1:15).

What is the image of God? Throughout the Bible we see that man carries certain characteristics in common with God. He has a soul, and he has a spirit that will continue to exist throughout eternity. Another characteristic man had at the beginning, but lost at the time of the fall, was the *moral* image of God. When Adam was created, he was perfect. When he sinned, he fell from that perfect state. This is clear in Genesis 5:3, which says Seth was created after Adam's image—the sinful image of his literal father. Because of Adam's transgression, sin entered the world (Romans 5:12). The moral image lost through the fall is regained only through the new birth. Colossians 3:10 reads: "And have put on the new man, which is renewed in knowledge after the image of him that created him."

Our faith in Christ makes us righteous and morally clean in God's sight. We are renewed in the image of God—the image man had at the time of creation.

Jesus was sinless and perfect and is the express image of God (Hebrews 1:3). Romans 8:29 tells us that the Lord has planned and purposed that we be conformed to the image of His Son. This is accomplished through faith and the new birth or regeneration of the Spirit of God. If we are in the image of the Son, we are in the image of God. Concerning our sinful state, we are perfect and sinless before

God. While in the flesh we are not exempt from sin, but our trust is in the righteousness of Christ, not our own righteousness or good works. However, as Christians we seek to live godly lives out of love for Christ and a desire to glorify our Redeemer.

16

How do you explain the Trinity?

There is little question that the Mormon church views the Christian doctrine of the Triune God as a false concept of the Deity. The *Teachings of the Prophet Joseph Smith* reads:

> Many men say there is one God; the Father, the Son and the Holy Ghost are only one God. I say that is a strange God anyhow— three in one, and one in three! It is a curious organization . . . All are crammed into one God, according to sectarianism. It would make the biggest God in all the world. He would be a wonderfully big God—he would be a giant or a monster. (*Teachings of the Prophet Joseph Smith*, p. 372)

During a speech at Brigham Young University on January 10, 1984, Mormon Apostle Bruce McConkie went so far as to say the Trinitarian view of God was the first and greatest heresy of Christianity. During the speech he said the doctrine of a three-in-one God filled the universe after Christ died and the adoption of the false image destroyed the true worship of God.

The truth that God the Father, the Son Jesus Christ, and the Holy Spirit are three distinct personages but *one* God was defined by the early church in the very precise Athanasian Creed. The creed reads in part:

> We worship one God in Trinity, and the Trinity in Unity; neither confounding the Persons: nor dividing the Substance [Essence]. For there is one Person of the Father: another of the Son: and another of the Holy Ghost. But the Godhead of the Father, of the Son, and of the Holy Ghost, is all one: the Glory equal, the Majesty

coeternal. Such as the Father is: such is the Son: and such is the Holy Ghost. The Father uncreate [uncreated]: the Son uncreate: and the Holy Ghost uncreate . . . the Father is Almighty: the Son Almighty: and the Holy Ghost Almighty. And yet they are not three Almighties: but one Almighty. So the Father is God: the Son is God: and the Holy Ghost is God. And yet they are not three Gods: but one God.

Because this creed was not written until the early fifth century, many Mormons claim this is a relatively new doctrine added to the Christian faith and was not a teaching of either Christ himself or His apostles.

But we need to understand that many of the creeds that represent the Christian faith were written to counter a prevailing heresy that had either attacked or infiltrated the Church. The doctrine of the Christian church was expressed through the precise language of a creed.

The Athanasian Creed was written to combat the false teachings of modalism and Arianism. Modalism has been given many other names throughout history. It was introduced around the third century in an attempt to preserve the doctrine of monotheism (belief in one God) as opposed to tri-theism, which taught the Godhead consisted of three separate Gods. In the attempt, proponents of modalism, Sabellius of Rome the most prominent, went to the other extreme by claiming the Father, Son, and Holy Ghost were merely three different *modes* of the same God, each revealing the same person.

Arianism got its name from Arius, the North African priest who was banished to Illyricum after his unorthodox teachings were condemned in A.D. 325 at the Council of Nicaea. He believed there was a time when Christ "was not," that Christ was essentially subordinate to the Father, a doctrine also held by Origen (ca.185–ca.254). While defenders of the triune concept of God held that Christ was of *one substance* with the Father but a distinct person, Arius held that Christ was of a *like substance*.

Mormonism and the Trinity

It is interesting to note that the *Book of Mormon* hints of modalism, while Mormonism today teaches a form of Arianism and tri-theism.

In the *Book of Mormon*, when the wicked lawyer Zeezrom asks Amulek if the Son of God is "the very eternal Father," the Nephite prophet says:

> Yea, he is the very Eternal Father of heaven and of earth, and all things which in them are. (Alma 11:39)

Occasionally I have heard Mormons say they believe in the Trinity, but I have found that they really mean they believe the Father, Son, and Holy Ghost are three separate Gods who make up the Godhead. Joseph Smith made this clear when he said:

> I will preach on the plurality of Gods. . . . I have always declared God to be a distinct personage, Jesus Christ a separate and distinct personage from God the Father, and that the Holy Ghost was a distinct personage and a spirit: and these three constitute three distinct personages and three Gods. (*Teachings of the Prophet Joseph Smith*, p. 370)

The Trinity in Scripture

Nowhere in the Scriptures do we read that there is more than one true God. The following verses are clear statements of the fact that only one God exists:

> Ye are my witnesses, saith the Lord, and my servant whom I have chosen; that ye may know and believe me, and understand that I am He: *before me there was no God formed, neither shall there be after me.* I, even I, am the Lord, and *beside me there is no savior*" (Isaiah 43:10–11; italics added).

> I am the first, and the last; *and beside me there is no God* (Isaiah 44:6; italics added).

> Is there a God besides me? yea, *there is no God; I know not any* (Isaiah 44:8; italics added).

> I am the Lord, *and there is none else, there is no God besides me.* (Isaiah 45:5; italics added)

> I am God, *and there is none else* (Isaiah 45:22; italics added).

> Remember the former things of old: for I am God, *and there is none else; I am God, and there is none like me* (Isaiah 46:9; italics added).

For there is *one God*, and one mediator between God and men, the man Christ Jesus (1 Timothy 2:5; italics added).

We know that an idol is nothing in the world, and that there is none *other God but one* (1 Corinthians 8:4; italics added).

Usually the Mormon will respond to such verses with a question about Mark 14:32–36, the passage about the Lord praying in the Garden of Gethsemane. Whom, the Mormons ask, was Jesus praying to?

The only way a person can understand Mark 14:32–36, even partially, is to accept the biblical fact that God is a spirit. Maintaining the false notion that God has a body of flesh and bones will lead to false conclusions.

Only a God of spirit can make the claim in Proverbs 15:3:

The eyes of the Lord are in every place, beholding the evil and the good.

We might understand the Trinity by three-part examples: Time— past, present, and future; Water—solid, liquid, and gas; The egg— shell, white and yolk. These examples may help us better understand the Trinitarian Godhead, but the infinite God is impossible to fully understand with the finite mind. However, just because the nature of the Trinity is difficult to understand does not mean it is not existent.

The Trinity in the *Book of Mormon*?

The Lord plainly declares in Scripture that there is no other God but He. It is surprising to realize that even the *Book of Mormon* supports a biblical view instead of Smith's claim that there are three Gods that make up the Godhead:

And now, behold, this is the doctrine of Christ, and the only true doctrine of the Father, and of the Son, and of the Holy Ghost, which is one God, without end. Amen. (2 Nephi 31:21)

But every thing shall be restored to its perfect frame, as it is now, or in the body, and shall be brought and be arraigned before the bar of Christ the Son, and God the Father, and the Holy Ghost, which is one eternal God. (Alma 11:44)

The Mormon church maintains that this description of one Triune

God is actually speaking of a God who is one in purpose. But to assume this thought is to read something into the *Book of Mormon* that is not there.

The *Book of Mormon* very strongly supports the idea that one God took upon himself the form of man and came to earth to redeem His people:

> And now Abinadi said unto them: I would that ye should understand the God Himself shall come down among the children of men, and shall redeem His people. (Mosiah 15:1)

> Have they not said that God Himself should come down among the children of men, and take upon Him the form of man, and go forth in mighty power upon the face of the earth. (Mosiah 13:34)

The *Book of Mormon* teaches against the plurality of Gods as taught by modern Mormonism. In the *Book of Mormon*, the story of the evil Zeezrom and righteous Amulek stresses monotheism:

> And Zeezrom said unto him [Amulek]: Thou sayest there is a true and living God? And Amulek said: Yea, there is a true and living God. Now Zeezrom said: Is there more than one God? And he answered, No. (Alma 11:26–29)

Not only is this in Smith's book, but Alma 11:22 tells us that Amulek would "say nothing which is contrary to the Spirit of the Lord."

Mormon apologist Roy W. Doxey attempts to explain away this passage by insisting the context refers to idolatry (*A Sure Foundation*, pp. 6–7). While we do find idolatry was a problem according to Alma 31, that was not the question Zeezrom asked of Amulek. He asked if there was only one "true and living God." If Amulek really believed there were others in existence (as taught later by Joseph Smith), why would he say there was only one? Isn't the Son a "true and living God"? Isn't the Holy Ghost a "true and living God"? If Amulek really believed in a plurality of Gods, as Mr. Doxey implies, why didn't he relate that to Zeezrom?

Discrepancy abounds. The LDS church preaches one doctrine and reads another out of its holy works. While it would be incorrect to charge the *Book of Mormon* with teaching a pure form of trinitarianism, it would be equally wrong to say it supports Mormon polytheism.

| 17 |

Didn't Paul support the doctrine of a plurality of gods in 1 Corinthians 8:5?

> For though there be that are called gods, whether in heaven or in earth, (as there be gods many, and lords many). (1 Corinthians 8:5)

Polytheism is the belief in, or worship of, many gods. Opposed to this dogma is *monotheism*, or belief in the existence of one God.

While many Mormons concede their faith teaches a view of more than one God, some detest being called polytheistic. This term, they say, brings to mind the thought of pagans worshiping at the altars of strange deities and idols. As strange as it may seem, many of these same people, while loathing the label "polytheist," will freely admit to believing in a plurality of gods. Semantics, however, does not erase the problem.

One big distinction that separated the Jews from their heathen counterparts was their persistent belief in the one God. The Scriptures make it clear that the only time this was not true was when the hearts of Israel turned against the God of Abraham, Isaac, and Jacob.

Monotheism in the Bible

No amount of scriptural gymnastics will alter the reality the Bible teaches explicitly in both Old and New Testaments—the concept of only one God. We find this teaching embedded in the Pentateuch (Deuteronomy 4:35; 6:4; 32:39). In Deuteronomy 4, Moses warns the children of Israel against the sin of idolatry and firmly declares:

> The Lord . . . is God; there is none else beside him.

Monotheism was proclaimed by King David as he sat before the Lord after being told by the prophet Nathan he was not to be the one to build the Temple for the Most High. In 2 Samuel 7:22 David says,

> Wherefore thou art great, O Lord God: for there is none like thee,

neither is there any God besides thee, according to all that we have heard with our ears.

In his psalms, David declares a belief in one God. Psalm 86:10 reads,

For thou art great, and doest wondrous things: thou art God alone.

One would be hard pressed to prove the prophet Isaiah believed in more than one God. In chapters 43–46 he proclaims no less than eleven times that there is only one God and that no others exist.

In an attempt to downplay Isaiah's pronouncements, Mormons have argued he was merely warning against idolatry. This defense is not only shallow, but irrational. The point Isaiah makes is that there are no other gods besides the true God—anywhere, or at any time.

If there did exist other gods on other worlds, as Mormons insist, certainly the omniscient God would know of them. Yet, Isaiah 44:8 plainly states the God of the Bible knows of no other Gods:

Is there a God besides me? yea, there is no God; I know not any.

When Jesus was asked of the scribes which is the first, or most important, commandment of all, He responded with a quote from the *Shema* found in Deuteronomy 6:4; again emphasizing monotheism. To this, one of the scribes said:

Well, master, thou hast said the truth: for there is one God; and there is none other but he. (Mark 12:32)

When Jesus heard this man's reply, He perceived that he had answered with understanding. Because he recognized the existence of only one true God, Jesus said he was not far from the kingdom of God (Mark 12:34). If Jesus said one is not far from the kingdom of God for believing in one God, it stands to reason that the one who believes in more than one God is not near the kingdom of God.

Paul and Monotheism

While addressing the early church at Corinth, the apostle Paul discussed the subject of idols and confirmed the monotheistic principle of Scripture:

> We know that an idol is nothing in the world, and that there is none other God but one. (1 Corinthians 8:4)

Mormons have attempted to nullify this interpretation by using the next verse:

> For though there be that are called gods, whether in heaven or in earth (as there be gods many and lords many).

This, they say, proves there is more than one God. In choosing this interpretation they ignore key words.

Notice Paul says "that are *called* gods." Sinful man has throughout history called many things gods, including trees, rocks, etc. Paul makes it clear in Galatians 4:8 that even though something is called a god, in reality it is not:

> Howbeit then, when ye knew not God, ye did service unto them which by nature are no gods.

In their unbelief they worshiped what they called gods, which were not gods at all. They were gods in their sin-darkened minds and not in reality.

Paul corrects any misconceptions in the verse that follows the reference to other gods:

> But to us there is but one God, the Father, of whom are all things, and we in him; and one Lord Jesus Christ, by whom are all things, and we by him. (1 Corinthians 8:6)

Mormon Polytheism

There is little question that Mormonism maintains the existence of more than one God. Brigham Young, the second prophet and president of the Mormon church, made this clear when he said:

> How many Gods there are, we do not know. But there never was a time when there were not Gods. (*Journal of Discourses*, 7:333)

The Pearl of Great Price, one of Mormonism's sacred books, contains a creation account in the *Book of Abraham*. Though it appears very similar to the creation account found in Genesis, one significant difference is readily seen. While Genesis states it was God (singular) who was responsible for the creation, chapter four in the *Book of*

Abraham states it was "the Gods," plural. These "Gods" are mentioned no less than 47 times within 31 verses.

Mormon Apostle Bruce R. McConkie explained his view of the Godhead in this fashion:

> Three separate personages—Father, Son, and Holy Ghost—comprise the Godhead. As each of these persons is a God, it is evident, from this standpoint alone, that a plurality of Gods exists. (*Mormon Doctrine*, p. 576)

In a quizzical twist McConkie also makes this statement in the same book:

> Polytheistic concepts are apostate versions of the original truth about God which was revealed to Adam and the ancient patriarchs . . . the saints [LDS] are not polytheists. (*Mormon Doctrine*, p. 579)

McConkie changes the definition of a polytheist. He insists that because Mormons claim to worship only the "Heavenly Father," they are exempt from this title. Bear in mind, however, polytheism is defined as the worship of, or belief in, more than one God. One cannot absolve himself of polytheism by merely holding a private definition of the word.

Worshiping Jesus

Mormons, though they claim to worship only the Father, come into disagreement over who may be worshiped. Elder Bernard P. Brockbank, while speaking at the 147th LDS General Conference in Salt Lake City, made this statement:

> It is true that many of the Christian churches worship a different Jesus Christ than is worshiped by the Mormons or Church of Jesus Christ of Latter-day Saints. . . . (*The Ensign*, May 1977, p. 26.)

Here, Mr. Brockbank makes it clear that the Jesus of Mormonism is indeed different than the Christian concept of Him. He also makes it clear that worship of this Jesus is perfectly acceptable. But the problem is that Jesus is considered by Mormons to be a distinct God, apart from the Father, not "one in essence" as affirmed by Trinitarian Christians.

Worship of Jesus is also taught in the *Book of Mormon*. Third Nephi 11:17 describes the Nephites calling Jesus the Most High God and worshiping Him.

To sidestep this apparent contradiction, Mr. McConkie takes it upon himself to redefine the word "worship" when it is used of Jesus. While giving a sermon at a BYU devotional on March 2, 1982, he said:

> I know perfectly well what the Scriptures say about worshiping Christ and Jehovah, but they are speaking in an entirely different sense—the sense of standing in awe and being reverentially grateful to him who redeemed us. (*Our Relationship With the Lord*, p. 5)

We cannot judge what he says in regard to the *Book of Mormon*, because we no longer have the original gold plates from which it was supposedly translated. As for the Bible, the same Greek word *proskuneo* is used when worship is given to the Father or the Son.

Shifting Theology

Those who have studied Joseph Smith's view of the Godhead quickly discover that his theology evolved drastically from 1830 to his death in 1844.

It is clear from what we read in the *Book of Mormon* that Smith maintained a belief in one God in the early 1830s. This thought is carried on into 1833 when Smith wrote his *Inspired Version* of the Bible. In fact, Smith used this new translation to "clarify" verses he thought implied the existence of more than one God. For example, the King James Version reads:

> And the Lord said unto Moses, See, I have made thee a god to Pharaoh. (Exodus 7:1)

Smith changed it to read,

> And the Lord said unto Moses, See, I have made thee a prophet to Pharaoh [sic]. (Exodus 7:1, JST)

We see this same pattern in Exodus 22:28. The King James Version reads:

> Thou shalt not revile the gods, nor curse the ruler of thy people.

Smith changed this to read,

> Thou shalt not revile against God, nor curse the ruler of thy
> people.

The second largest splinter group of Latter-day Saints, the Reorganized Church of Jesus Christ of Latter-day Saints, denounces any such notion that their founder Joseph Smith taught a plurality of Gods. In defense of this position they point to the *Book of Mormon*, the *Doctrine and Covenants*, and the *Inspired Version* verses cited above.

In his booklet *The Truth and the Evidence*, Reorganized Apostle Aleah G. Koury defends the RLDS position of monotheism by stating:

> It is noteworthy that in the three standard scriptures of the
> church, the *Book of Mormon*, the Book of *Doctrine and Covenants*,
> and the *Inspired Version* of the Holy Scriptures, particular empha-
> sis is laid on the fact that there is only one God who ever was or
> ever will exist. . . . It therefore becomes unreasonable to suggest
> that he [Joseph Smith] would ever attempt to promulgate a doc-
> trine of plural gods in complete opposition to the divinely revealed
> concept revealed for the church. (*The Truth and Evidence*, p. 21)

The sources of authority for the LDS in Utah and the RLDS in Independence, Missouri, have been contested since Joseph Smith's death in 1844. It is doubtful these two groups will ever come to terms. Nonetheless, the Utah Mormons, from their own assertions, have clearly separated themselves from monotheism. Mormonism falls into the same category as Hinduism, Taoism, Shintoism, and various African tribal religions, as well as ancient religions of the Greeks, Romans, Babylonians, and Assyrians. Their claim to be a restoration of historical Christianity is groundless. Whether Mormons wish to be called polytheists or not is really of little significance since they assail the biblical message of monotheism.

18

If God is a spirit, why did Moses say he saw God face-to-face?

And the Lord spake unto Moses face to face, as a man speaketh unto his friend. (Exodus 33:11)

By failing to recognize two very important verses in the thirty-third chapter of Exodus, the Mormon draws the very wrong conclusion that God has a body of flesh and bones.

What Moses saw was a *theophany*, the invisible God taking on a form His creation could see. Theophanies are mentioned many times throughout the Bible.

The book of Hebrews says:

By faith he [Moses] forsook Egypt, not fearing the wrath of the king: for he endured as seeing him who is invisible. (Hebrews 11:27)

This was accomplished by the invisible God taking on a visible form; by way of a theophany.

Mormons fail to acknowledge Exodus 33:9–20. Verse 20 says that no man can see God's face and live. This may at first seem to contradict verse 11. But verse 9 clarifies the controversy:

And it came to pass, as Moses entered in the tabernacle, the cloudy pillar descended, and stood at the door of the tabernacle, and the Lord talked with Moses.

The Lord talked with Moses face-to-face through the cloudy pillar, the same way He talked to Moses from the burning bush. Both times Moses saw the theophany, yet never actually saw God's person, for He is invisible.

To understand this phenomenon, imagine talking to someone in the dark. You can't actually see the person to whom you are speaking, but there is no doubt by the sound of the voice that you are speaking with the person face-to-face.

Joseph Smith Sees God

Joseph Smith claimed one could see God *if* he held the Mormon priesthood:

> And without the ordinances thereof, and the authority of the priesthood, the power of godliness is not manifest unto men in the flesh; For without this no man can see the face of God, even the Father, and live. (*Doctrine and Covenants*, 84:21–22)

His statement is intriguing because Joseph Smith had no such priesthood in 1820, the year he claimed to have seen God. Mormon apologists have attempted to sidestep this perplexing problem by pointing to people who had visions of Jesus Christ, yet held no priestly authority (such as Saul on the road to Damascus). They reason that since Jesus is a God and was seen of men, it is not really necessary to have the priesthood. Such reasoning does a great disservice to the English language.

The book *A Sure Foundation* quotes Melvin J. Petersen, professor of LDS church history and doctrine at Brigham Young University. Mr. Petersen uses John 14:23 as a proof text that man can see God (p. 79). But this is an odd verse to use because it has nothing at all to do with men seeing God with their eyes, as Smith claimed he had.

Mr. Petersen points to John 1:18 of the *Joseph Smith Translation* to support his claim.

> No man hath seen God at any time, *except* he hath borne record of the Son. (italics added)

Here we find Joseph Smith purposely altered the scripture to support his heretical teaching. No Greek manuscript supports such a clear example of perverting Scripture. Yet, it is to this kind of argument Mormons must retreat. John 1:18 correctly reads:

> No man hath seen God at any time; the only begotten Son, which is in the bosom of the Father, he hath declared him.

The context clearly shows that God the Father has been seen by no man at any time. Yet it was the Father that Smith claimed to have seen in 1820. Scripture proves him wrong.

19

How do you explain Jeremiah 1:5 if you don't believe in the preexistence of the soul?

Before I formed thee in the belly I knew thee; and before thou camest forth out of the womb I sanctified thee, and I ordained thee a prophet unto the nations. (Jeremiah 1:5)

Mormons believe we all existed as spirit children with God in heaven, waiting to take on a physical body. When someone on earth gives birth to a child, one of these spirit children leaves heaven to dwell in that physical body. The spirit child loses all remembrance of his time in heaven when he possesses the physical body. Mormonism teaches there is a heavenly mother, God's wife, who births these spirit children through a physical relationship with God the Father.

This scenario defies common sense. Since Mormons believe God has a body of flesh and bones, they also believe the heavenly mother has a body of flesh and bones. Thus two fleshly personages procreate spirit children. Common sense—as well as Genesis 1—tells us that like kinds create like kinds. A heavenly mother and father having flesh and bones should be having physical children in heaven, not spiritual.

The preexistence of spirit children clearly contradicts Bible teaching. Zechariah 12:1 says God forms the spirit of man within man, not in a heavenly mother. The spirit of man is formed within him at the time of creation by God; when that man dies, his spirit returns to the One who placed it in him.

To support the doctrine of preexistence, Brigham Young taught in 1852:

We were made first spiritual, and afterwards temporal. (*Journal of Discourses*, 1:50)

The Bible says just the opposite:

Howbeit that was not first which is spiritual, but that which is natural; and afterward that which is spiritual. (1 Corinthians 15:46)

The next three verses (1 Corinthians 15:47–49) tell us that we now have an earthly body but shall later put on the heavenly, or incorruptible body, that will last for eternity.

The passage in Jeremiah is not referring to the preexistence of man, but rather to the foreknowledge of God. Before Jeremiah was born, God knew he would become a prophet.

> God . . . calleth those things which be not as though they were. (Romans 4:17)

What about Ezekiel 37:16–17? Doesn't this prove the forthcoming of the Book of Mormon?

Ezekiel 37:16–17 says:

> Moreover thou son of man, take thee one stick, and write upon it, for Judah, and for the children of Israel his companions: then take another stick, and write upon it, for Joseph, the stick of Ephraim, and for all the house of Israel his companions; and join them one to another into one stick; and they shall become one in thine hand.

In the book, *A Marvelous Work and a Wonder*, Mormon Apostle LeGrand Richards attempts to use Ezekiel 37:16–20 as a proof text that the Bible predicts the coming forth of Joseph Smith's *Book of Mormon.*

Richards states:

> In ancient times it was the custom to write on parchment and roll it on a stick. Therefore, when this command was given, it was the equivalent of directing that two books or records should be kept. . . . Could this promise be fulfilled in a more simple and perfect manner than it was through the coming forth of the Book of Mormon. (*A Marvelous Work and a Wonder,* pp. 67–68)

This interpretation also appears in the Mormon church publication, *Meet the Mormons*:

> Because some ancient records were kept on parchment or other material and rolled on sticks, they were referred to as "sticks." (p. 45)

In early times when parchments were wrapped around sticks, they were called scrolls. To interpret these verses in Ezekiel 37 in such a way is to do a great injustice to the Hebrew language in which they were written.

The Hebrew word for "stick" is *aits*, literally, a stick or a piece of wood, *not* a scroll as Mormon authorities imply. In Ezekiel 24:10, the word *aits* is translated as wood. In many other portions of the Old Testament it is translated as timber.

Had Ezekiel meant records or scrolls, he would have used the correct Hebrew word, which is *saipher*. Since he did not, it cannot be assumed that the Mormon interpretation is correct.

Had LeGrand Richards not stopped with verse 20, but gone on to verse 22 he would have seen that Ezekiel was not referring to scrolls at all. Verse 22 shows what the sticks represented:

> And I will make them one nation in the land upon the mountains of Israel; and one king shall be king to them all: and they shall be no more two nations, neither shall they be divided into two kingdoms any more at all.

The sticks Ezekiel was told to write on represented Israel and Judah. Ever since the reign of King Rehoboam, the kingdom had been divided into these two warring nations. Now God was telling His prophet Ezekiel that He had plans to bring them back together again—they were going to be one nation once more.

This prophecy was partially fulfilled when the children of Israel left Babylon after the captivity, but will be totally fulfilled when Jesus Christ reigns as the one King over all.

Mormons also claim the twenty-ninth chapter of Isaiah speaks of the forthcoming *Book of Mormon*. The verses they refer to say:

> And the vision of all is become unto you as the words of a book that is sealed, which men deliver to one that is learned, saying, Read this, I pray thee: and he saith, I cannot; for it is sealed. . . . There-

fore, behold, I will do a marvelous work among this people, even a marvelous work and a wonder . . . (Isaiah 29:11–14).

A close examination of this chapter reveals that it is referring to the nation of Israel and has nothing whatsoever to do with the Mormon movement or the *Book of Mormon*.

Isaiah 29 is a warning to God's people. The people of Israel had such favor in God's eyes that He sent His prophets to personally give them the Word of God. Because of their hardheartedness they couldn't tell which prophets were of God and which were not. God refers to their lack of discernment as trying to read a book that is sealed (29:11). Jerusalem, the proud city, would be distressed and brought low, humbled so low that God said their "speech shall whisper out of the dust" (29:4).

Mormons believe the "marvelous work and wonder" is the *Book of Mormon*. The Bible says this marvelous work would be from among their people (the Jews). The marvelous work and wonder is Jesus Christ and His ministry here on earth.

LeGrand Richards, on page 69 of his book, says,

> Their speech would be low out of the dust; their voice would be as a familiar spirit, out of the ground; their speech would whisper out of the dust. Now, obviously, the only way a dead people could speak "out of the ground" or "low out of the dust" would be by a written word, *and this the people did through the Book of Mormon. Truly it has a familiar spirit,* for it contains the words of the prophets of the God of Israel.

It is interesting that Mr. Richards connects familiar spirits with the Book of Mormon. Every time the phrase "familiar spirit(s)" is used in the Bible it is used in connection with witchcraft and the occult. For example, Leviticus 19:31 warns us to *"Regard them not that have familiar spirits,* neither seek after wizards, to be defiled by them: I am the Lord your God."

Leviticus 20:6 says, "the soul that turneth after such as have familiar spirits, and after wizards, to go a whoring after them" will be cut off from among the people.

Leviticus 20:27 says that "A man also or a woman that hath a familiar spirit . . . *shall surely be put to death."*

Deuteronomy 18:11 says a "consulter with familiar spirits" is an abomination unto the Lord.

Second Kings 21:6 states that one of the reasons Manasseh was considered a wicked king was because he "dealt with familiar spirits."

First Chronicles 10:13 states that "King Saul died for his transgressions which he committed against the Lord." One of those transgressions was that he sought "counsel of one that had a familiar spirit" (the witch at Endor).

Mr. Richards assumes the people speaking out of the dust are all dead. The Scripture does not say that. It merely says they will be distressed and have sorrow—not that there would be a total annihilation. Neither is there any indication of a great time span between verses three and four, which would hint that any survivors would have died. Rather, the humbling effect would take place immediately following the siege mentioned in verse three.

So what is Isaiah saying? He means Jerusalem would be made to grovel in the dust at the feet of their captors. When he says "their voice shall be as one that has a familiar spirit" he speaks of a voice that is faint and feeble, a "ghost-like expression that is low key, not boastful and loud." Having a familiar spirit was punishable by death and those who dealt with them whispered in fear lest they be found out and executed. Such would be the same for this conquered city.

21

Who is the Ancient of Days if it isn't Adam as Joseph Smith taught?

Joseph Smith taught:

> Daniel in his seventh chapter speaks of the Ancient of Days; he means the oldest man, our Father Adam, Michael, he will call his children together and hold a counsel with them to prepare them for the coming of the Son of Man. (*Teachings of the Prophet Joseph Smith*, p. 157)

However, a close examination of the seventh chapter of Daniel will tell precisely who the Ancient of Days is. Daniel writes:

> I beheld till the thrones were cast down, and the Ancient of days did sit, whose garment was white as snow, and the hair of his head like the pure wool: his throne was like the fiery flame, and his wheels as burning fire. (Daniel 7:9)

> One like the Son of Man came with the clouds of heaven, and came to the Ancient of days, and they brought him near before him. And there was given him [the one who was brought before the Ancient of days] dominion, and glory, and a kingdom, that all people, nations, and languages, should serve him. (Daniel 7:13–14)

From this passage we see that the Ancient of Days is God the Father. John 5:22 tells us that the Father has committed all judgment unto the Son:

> For the Father judgeth no man, but hath committed all judgment unto the Son.

These passages parallel Revelation 5:1–7, in which John in his vision sees God the Father sitting on the throne holding a scroll sealed with seven seals. A strong angel cries out wondering who can open the sealed scroll (v. 2). Verses 6 and 7 tell us that the Lamb comes forth and takes the sealed scroll from the hand of Him who sits on the throne. The Lamb is the Son of God, Jesus Christ, who is worthy to open the seals.

Adam as the Ancient of Days

Joseph Smith taught that Adam was the Ancient of Days while the Bible teaches the Ancient of Days is God. Put the two teachings together, and Adam becomes God. This makes it easier to understand why Brigham Young got his doctrinal wires crossed when he taught that Adam was really God. Here is what Brigham Young taught on April 9, 1852:

> Now hear it, O inhabitants of the earth, Jew and Gentile, Saint and sinner! When our Father Adam came into the Garden of Eden, he came into it with a celestial body, and brought Eve, one of his wives, with him. He helped to make and organize this world. He is Michael, the Archangel, the *Ancient of Days!* about whom holy men have written and spoken—He is our Father and our God, and the *only God with whom we have to do.* (*Journal of Discourses*, 1:50)

Brigham Young espouses many biblical and logical errors in this statement:

- Adam did not come into the Garden of Eden with a celestial body—he had an earthly body (1 Corinthians 15:45–49).
- Adam did not bring Eve with him for Eve was created after Adam (Genesis 2:20–23).
- The Bible refers to Eve as being Adam's *only* wife, not one of his wives.
- Adam did not help in the creation of this world; he was part of that creation (Genesis 1:26–31).
- Adam cannot possibly be Michael the Archangel, nor the Ancient of Days.

Adam Is God

Daniel proclaims God the Father to be the Ancient of Days. If Brigham Young insists that Adam is the same Ancient of Days, he must believe it is Adam who sits on the throne when Jesus comes to take the sealed scroll in Revelation 5:7. To this day Mormons teach that Adam is the Ancient of Days. So whether they readily admit it or not, they are still teaching that Adam is God! McConkie states in *Mormon Doctrine*, "Adam is known as the Ancient of Days" (p. 34). Also, in *Doctrine and Covenants* we find, "and also with Michael, or Adam, the father of all, the prince of all, the ancient of days" (p. 47).

For years, Mormon apologists have been trying to persuade people that Brigham Young did not believe that Adam was God. They claim he was misquoted or misunderstood. But in light of all the documents to prove the contrary, this is a weak argument.

On December 10, 1853, more than a year after the first Adam-God sermon was recorded, the same teaching was printed in the Mormon *Millennial Star*. It was entitled "Adam, the Father and God of the Human Family." The article stated, "Adam is really God! And why not?" (*Millennial Star*, 15:801). Mr. Young had more than a year to change any misquotes before this appeared. Obviously, he felt there was nothing to correct.

To say the Adam-God teaching was just an idea Brigham Young had and shouldn't be taken as true doctrine is also a weak argument. He claimed in 1870 that he had never delivered a sermon among men that they might not call scripture (*Journal of Discourses*, 13:95). In the *Desert News*, June 14, 1873, Young claimed God revealed the doctrine to him.

Mormon apologists claim Young's assertions cannot be considered true doctrine because he didn't say "Thus saith the Lord" before he commenced this sermon. While this may seem to get the Mormon prophet off the hook, it is not consistent with LDS policy. Ezra Taft Benson said that the prophet speaks as the mouthpiece of God, and he does not have to precede his message with "Thus saith the Lord" (*Ogden Standard Examiner*, p. 2A, Feb. 26, 1980). This concurs with Mormon General Authority J. Reuben Clark, Jr.:

> There are those who insist that unless the Prophet of the Lord declares, "Thus saith the Lord," the message may not be taken as a revelation. This is a false testing standard. For while many of our modern revelations as contained in the *Doctrine and Covenants* do contain these words, there are many that do not. (*Living Prophets for a Living Church*, p. 68.)

The evidence says that Brigham Young was not misunderstood. There are too many documents that prove Young meant exactly what he said. Heber C. Kimball, one of the first presidents under Brigham Young, declared:

> The first man sent his own Son to redeem the world, to redeem his brethren; his life was taken, his blood shed, that our sins might be remitted. That Son called twelve men and ordained them to be Apostles, and when he departed the keys of the kingdom were deposited with three of those twelve, viz: Peter, James, and John. (*Journal of Discourses*, 4:1)

An honest Mormon will admit that the "first man" was none other than Adam. Kimball's statement parallels that of Young four years earlier when Young declared:

> When the Virgin Mary conceived the child Jesus, the Father had begotten him in his own likeness. He was not begotten by the Holy Ghost. And who is the Father? He is the first of the human family. . . . Jesus, our elder brother, was begotten in the flesh by the same character that was in the garden of Eden, and who is our Father in heaven. Now let all who may hear these doctrines, pause before they make light of them, or treat them with indifference, for

they will prove their salvation or damnation. (*Journal of Discourses,* 1:50–51)

It is interesting to learn that Spencer Kimball, the twelfth president of the LDS church, claimed Brigham's "alleged" teachings were false doctrine:

> We warn you against the dissemination of doctrines which are not according to the Scriptures and which are alleged to have been taught by some of the General Authorities of past generations. Such, for instance is the Adam-God theory.
> We denounce that theory and hope that everyone will be cautioned against this and other kinds of false doctrine. (*Church News,* Oct. 9, 1976)

Evidence clearly shows that the doctrine was taught and not alleged. Either Brigham Young is a false prophet for teaching this doctrine, or Spencer Kimball is a false prophet for denying it. Both claim to be prophets of God, yet both disagree as to who God is.

Although Spencer Kimball is correct (the Adam-God doctrine is a false teaching), Kimball's statement that this teaching was "alleged" casts severe doubt on his credibility. It is hard to believe the twelfth prophet of the Mormon church was totally ignorant of all the available evidence that proves that the second prophet of the church taught and believed this heretical doctrine.

Mormons hold firmly to their doctrine of the Godhead. Mormon Apostle Bruce McConkie told one group that salvation depends upon a right conception of the Godhead:

> There is no salvation in believing any false doctrine, particularly a false or unwise view about the Godhead or any of its members. (*Our Relationship With the Lord,* p. 2)

As he denies the Adam-God doctrine, consistency would demand McConkie to conclude Brigham Young was not saved or deny the reality of the evidence.

lead me." I was trying to think of the place where God is not, but it is impossible, unless you can find *empty* space; and *there* I believe He is not. If you can find such a place, it will become useful for a hiding place to those who wish to hide themselves from the presence of the Lord, in the great day of accounts. I will close this sermon, as I intend to preach another before I present the subject I more particularly wish to speak upon. My next sermon will be to both Saint and sinner. One thing has remained a mystery in this kingdom up to this day. It is in regard to the character of the well-beloved Son of God, upon which subject the Elders of Israel have conflicting views. Our God and Father in heaven, is a being of tabernacle, or, in other words, He has a body, with parts the same as you and I have; and is capable of showing forth His works to organized beings, as, for instance, in the world in which we live, it is the result of the knowledge and infinite wisdom that dwell in His organized body. His son Jesus Christ has become a personage of tabernacle, and has a body like his father. The Holy Ghost is the Spirit of the Lord, and issues forth from Himself, and may properly be called God's minister to execute His will in immensity; being called to govern by His influence and power; but *He* is not a person of tabernacle as we are, and as our Father in Heaven and Jesus Christ are. The question has been, and is often, asked, who it was that begat the Son of the Virgin Mary. The infidel world would have concluded that if what the Apostles wrote about his father and mother be true, and the present marriage discipline acknowledged by Christendom be correct, then Christians must believe that God is the father of an illegitimate son, in the person of Jesus Christ! The infidel fraternity teach *that* to their disciples. I will tell you how it is. Our Father in Heaven begat all the spirits that ever were, or ever will be, upon this earth; and they were born spirits in the eternal world. Then the Lord by His power and wisdom organized the mortal tabernacle of man. We were made first spiritual, and afterwards temporal.

Now hear it, O inhabitants of the earth, Jew and Gentile, Saint and sinner! When our father Adam came into the garden of Eden, he came into it with a *celestial body*, and brought Eve, *one of his wives*, with him. He helped to make and organize this world. He is MICHAEL, *the Archangel*, the ANCIENT OF DAYS! about whom holy men have written and spoken — HE *is our* FATHER *and our* GOD, *and the only God with whom* WE *have to do*. Every man upon the earth, professing Christians or nonprofessing, must hear it, and *will know it sooner or later*. They came here, organized the raw material, and arranged in their order the herbs of the field, the trees, the apple, the peach, the plum, the pear, and every other fruit that is desirable and good for man; the seed was brought from another sphere, and planted in this earth. The thistle, the thorn, the brier, and the obnoxious weed did *not* appear until after the earth was cursed. When Adam and Eve had eaten of the forbidden fruit, their bodies became mortal from *its effects*, and therefore their offspring were mortal. When the Virgin Mary conceived the child Jesus, the Father had begotten him in his own likeness. He was *not* begotten by the Holy Ghost. And who is the Father? He is the first of the human family; and when he took a tabernacle, it was begotten by *his Father* in heaven, after the same manner as the tabernacles of Cain, Abel, and the rest of the sons and daughters of Adam and Eve; from the fruits of the earth, the first earthly tabernacles were originated by the Father, and so

---

On April 9, 1852, Brigham Young preached probably the most controversial sermon of his lifetime. He claimed Adam was God and the "only God with

SELF-GOVERNMENT—MYSTERIES—ETC.

on in succession. I could tell you much more about this ; but were I to tell you the whole truth, blasphemy would be nothing to it, in the estimation of the superstitious and over-righteous of mankind. However, I have told you the truth as far as I have gone. I have heard men preach upon the divinity of Christ, and exhaust all the wisdom they possessed. All Scripturalists, and approved theologians who were considered exemplary for piety and education, have undertaken to expound on this subject, in every age of the Christian era ; and after they have done all, they are obliged to conclude by exclaiming "great is the mystery of godliness." and tell nothing.

It is true that the earth was organized by three distinct characters, namely, Elohcim, Yahovah, and Michael, these three forming a quorum, as in all heavenly bodies, and in organizing element, perfectly represented in the Deity, as Father, Son, and Holy Ghost.

Again, they will try to tell how the divinity of Jesus is joined to his humanity, and exhaust all their mental faculties, and wind up with this profound language, as describing the soul of man, "it is an immaterial substance ! " What a learned idea ! Jesus, our elder brother, was begotten in the flesh by the same character that was in the garden of Eden, and who is our Father in Heaven. Now, let all who may hear these doctrines, pause before they make light of them, or treat them with indifference, for they will prove their salvation or damnation.

I have given you a few leading items upon this subject, but a great deal more remains to be told. Now, remember from this time forth, and for ever, that Jesus Christ was not begotten by the Holy Ghost. I will repeat a little anecdote. I was in conversation with a certain learned professor upon this subject, when I replied, to this idea—" if the Son was begotten by the Holy Ghost, it would be very dangerous to baptize and confirm females, and give the Holy Ghost to them, lest he should beget children, to be palmed upon the Elders by the people, bringing the Elders into great difficulties."

Treasure up these things in your hearts. In the Bible, you have read the things I have told you to-night ; but you have not known what you did read. I have told you no more than you are conversant with ; but what do the people in Christendom, with the Bible in their hands, know about this subject ? Comparatively nothing.

I will now again take up the subject of tithing. The brethren have done well. They have been willing and obedient, no people could have been more so ; for this I thank my Father in Heaven. I could not wish a people to work more kindly in the yoke of Jesus than this people do ; the yoke grows more and more easy to them. It seems that every man will not only pay his tithing, but give all he has, if the Lord requires it : still I see wherein they may do better. I asked the people to day to assist to pay our Church liabilities. The offer of three or four yoke of oxen only, we do not want ; but I will lay before you what we wish you to do. By the manifesto which has been read, you have learned the precise situation ‘of the property of the Church. What has incurred this debt ? Why does it exist in the shape in which it now appears ? And wherein could we have obviated the difficulty, and done better ? A fourth part of the money already paid out, did not come in upon tithing. This money we have had to borrow in order to keep the public works in progress. You may say, wherein could we have done better, for we have paid our tithing punctually ? But has that brother, who sent $100 back to the

---

22

How do you interpret John 3:5 if you don't think "born of water" means baptism?

In John 3:5, Jesus says to Nicodemus:

> Verily, verily, I say unto thee, Except a man be born of water and of the Spirit, he cannot enter into the kingdom of God.

It is much simpler to understand what Jesus was saying to Nicodemus if we take verses 5 and 6 together. By reading these passages in context, it appears that our Lord is talking about physical birth and spiritual birth. The spiritual new birth can only take place if one has first been born physically. Nicodemus understood what Jesus was saying about the physical birth, for he states:

> How can a man be born when he is old? Can he enter the second time into his mother's womb, and be born? (John 3:4)

If you have ever witnessed the birth of a child, you will understand what Jesus meant by being "born of water." Babies are literally born in water.

The first birth is physical, the second is spiritual. Unless a man is born again—born spiritually—he will not enter into the kingdom of heaven. Notice that the word baptism isn't even mentioned here by Jesus.

Baptism cannot be a requirement for salvation because Christ's blood saves us, not water (Ephesians 1:7). Also, baptism is something we do, a *work* (Ephesians 2:8–9). Baptism of the believer should be performed as a sign that the convert has made the decision to follow Christ, but it cannot do anything to help us gain salvation.

To say baptism is absolutely essential is to deny the many passages that show works are not a requirement for salvation.

Mormons also use 1 Peter 3:20–21 to support their claim that you must be baptized to enter heaven:

> Which sometime were disobedient, when once the longsuffering of God waited in the days of Noah, while the ark was a preparing,

wherein few, that is, eight souls were saved by water. The like figure whereunto even baptism doth also now save us.

What they fail to realize is that the last half of verse 21 makes everything clear:

Not the putting away of the filth of the flesh [which is what water does], but the answer of a good conscience toward God, by the resurrection of Jesus Christ.

In the context of baptism, it is good to note that it was Noah and his family who were dry and stayed alive; the wet ones died outside the protection of the ark.

23

Who are the other sheep Jesus talked about in John 10:16?

And other sheep I have, which are not of this fold: them also I must bring, and they shall hear my voice; and there shall be one fold, and one shepherd. (John 10:16)

Mormonism claims Jesus was referring to a group of people known as the Nephites and Lamanites when he spoke of these "other sheep." However, neither history nor archaeology gives any indication that either group ever existed. Not even intelligent Mormon anthropologists will stick their necks out and say they can prove this:

Many times, Mormon missionaries have told their investigators that such late-period ruins as Monte-Alban (periods III–V), Yagul, and Mitla were built by the Nephites and that archaeologists would confirm this. Both claims are untrue. (Joseph E. Vincent, *University Archaeological Society Newsletter*, No. 66, May 7, 1960, p. 2)

Mormon anthropologist Ross T. Christensen stated:

The statement that the *Book of Mormon* has already been proved by archaeology is misleading. (*U.A.S. Newsletter*, No. 64, January 30, 1960)

Mormon anthropologist Dr. John L. Sorenson, who is Professor Emeritus of anthropology at Brigham Young University, said:

> As long as Mormons generally are willing to be fooled by (and pay for) the uninformed, uncritical drivel about archeology and the Scriptures which predominates, the few LDS experts are reluctant even to be identified with the topic. (*Dialogue, A Journal of Mormon Thought*, Spring 1966, pp. 145–146)

Sunstone magazine included an article by LDS art historian Martin Raish. *Sunstone* is considered a liberal Mormon publication that has been known to be much more objective than the Mormon church would like to be on certain subjects. Entitled "All that Glitters: Uncovering Fool's Gold in *Book of Mormon* Archaeology," Mr. Raish castigates zealous Mormons who insist that archaeological discoveries in South and Central America vindicate the *Book of Mormon* story. Raish admits that many of the quotes used to verify *Book of Mormon* archaeology are taken out of context and gives examples to prove his point (*Sunstone*, January/February 1981, p. 11).

Two classic examples of erroneous information would be *The Americas Before Columbus* by Dewey Farnsworth and *The Book of Mormon on Trial* by Jack West. These books so inaccurately portray the truth that John Sorenson wrote in a private letter dated October 5, 1981, that they were "worse than useless because they are not reasonably close to the truth." In spite of the concern he expresses, in April 1990 while I was visiting various LDS sites around Palmyra, New York, I was surprised to see *The Book of Mormon on Trial* still displayed on the shelf at the Palmyra LDS bookstore.

The Mormon church is also guilty of actively perpetrating the lie that the *Book of Mormon* has been proven with concrete evidence. One edition of *Meet the Mormons* reads:

> But as archaeology and anthropology began to explore these areas, the *Book of Mormon* claims—fantastic as some once thought them to be—were soon substantiated with concrete physical evidence. . . . The vast discoveries and extensive research of recent

years verify the *Book of Mormon* story. (*Meet the Mormons* 1965 ed., p. 40)

The *Book of Mormon* states that the early inhabitants of the American continent were of Hebrew descent. But Mesoamerican archaeologist Michael Coe wrote in the *Biblical Archaeology Review*:

> It would be difficult to find a trained archaeologist who is not a Mormon who believes that the Mesoamerican Indians are descendants of the Israelites. (September/October 1985 issue of *Biblical Archaeology Review*)

The Bible does tell us who these *other sheep* are. They are not the Nephites nor the Lamanites, but are instead the Gentiles. The Lord Jesus made it clear that the Gospel would first be given to the Jews. Because of their unbelief it was later delivered to the Gentiles (Acts 28:28). This commission to preach to the Gentile people was given to Paul according to Acts 9:15. Now when either Jews or Gentiles embrace Jesus Christ as Lord and Savior, they are no longer separated by their former titles but are of one fold—Christians.

Romans 10 illustrates the fact that the Gentiles are the other sheep:

> But I say, Did not Israel know? First Moses saith, I will provoke you to jealousy by them that are no people, and by a foolish nation will I anger you. But Esaias is very bold, and saith, I was found of them that sought me not; I was manifest unto them that asked not after me. (Romans 10:19–20)

Neither the Nephites nor the Lamanites can meet this qualification. By every definition of the word, the *Book of Mormon* story and the people it speaks of are nothing more than myth.

| 24 |

Doesn't Jesus say that men may become gods in John 10:34?

> Jesus answered them, Is it not written in your law, I said, Ye are gods? (John 10:34)

This verse and the Mormon doctrine of men becoming gods are inconsistent. For one thing, our Lord uses the present tense: "Is it not written in your law, I said, Ye *are* gods?" Not even Mormonism embraces the teaching that Mormon men are gods *now*, rather they teach that men will not become gods until the next life.

Furthermore, Jesus could not have been hinting that men could become God like him, since that would be in direct contradiction to Scripture, and the Lord himself said, "The scripture cannot be broken" (John 10:35).

Isaiah 43:10 makes it quite clear that the Lord is the only God and that there never will be any other:

> Ye are my witnesses, saith the Lord, and my servant whom I have chosen: that ye may know and believe Me, and understand that I am He: before me there was no God formed, neither shall there be after me.

By this word we have the authority that no one—not Joseph Smith, Brigham Young, or any other Mormon—will ever be a god.

The Mormon who insists on his attaining godhood should be alerted to Jeremiah 10:10–11:

> But the Lord is the true God, he is the living God, and an everlasting king: at his wrath the earth shall tremble, and the nations shall not be able to abide His indignation. Thus shall ye say unto them, the gods that have not made the heavens and the earth, even they shall perish from the earth, and from under these heavens.

It may be argued that this verse refers to pagan idols. Though that may be the case, let us remember that according to Psalm 96:5, God considers all the gods of the nations to be idols, whether they are hewn from wood or stone or "exalted" through good works, as is taught in the Mormon church. All who hold to such a concept will perish.

While Mormon Apostle James Talmage discusses John 10:34 in his book *Jesus the Christ*, few Mormons today use him as a resource. This may be because he refutes their preconceived notion. He writes:

> Divinely Appointed Judges Called "gods": In Psalm 82:6, judges invested by divine appointment are called "gods." To this the Savior referred in His reply to the Jews in Solomon's Porch. (*Jesus the Christ*, p. 501)

The "gods" our Lord refers to are humans who have been divinely appointed to rule over the people. Though a Mormon may argue that the word used in this passage is *Elohim* (the same word used to describe God himself), we find other instances where the context demands that its meaning has nothing to do with deity.

Exodus 21:6 is an example of this. It reads that when a servant wishes to be indentured for life, they must "bring him unto the judges." The word for judges is the Hebrew *Elohim*.

The Hebrew *Elohim* is used again in Exodus 22:8, where it says that when a man's goods are entrusted to another and are stolen by an unknown thief, "both parties shall come before the judges." In both these cases the context does not allow the use of this word to refer to deity, but rather men appointed to rule over the people.

If we look closely at Psalm 82, from which Jesus quoted, we discover this psalm is a rebuke against rulers who have abused their authority (just as those whom our Lord addresses in John 10:34). For their sins they shall die like men (v. 7). If the Mormon interpretation is preferred, then it also must be assumed that gods die. This would not be consistent with their doctrine, because the Mormon view of becoming a god includes immortality—and how could an immortal being die?

25

Doesn't 1 John 3:2 say we will be like Jesus, proving we will be gods?

> Beloved, now are we the sons of God, and it doth not yet appear what we shall be: but we know that, when he shall appear, we shall be like him; for we shall see him as he is. (1 John 3:2)

The resurrected Christian shall indeed be like his Savior, but to assume this means *godhood* is to believe something Scripture does not support.

Isaiah 43:10 states plainly:

> Before me there was no God formed, neither shall there be *after* me [italics added].

We shall share heaven, eternal joy, and immortality with Christ. First Corinthians 15:53 tells us, "For this corruptible must put on incorruption, and this mortal must put on immortality."

By faith we are now the sons and daughters of God. We are joint-heirs with Christ according to Romans 8:17, and will be glorified together with Him. The Scriptures only hint as to what that glory will be. First Corinthians 2:9 says:

> But as it is written, Eye hath not seen, nor ear heard, neither have entered into the heart of man, the things which God hath prepared for them that love him.

We stand in awe of what God will make us, but we know we will *always* stand in awe of the Savior who made it possible for us to go to heaven with Him. No matter how exalted a position we receive, His glory and majesty will always be beyond anything He can give us, because He alone is God.

26

Doesn't 2 Corinthians 12:2 prove there are three degrees of glory?

I knew a man in Christ above fourteen years ago, (whether in the body, I cannot tell; or whether out of the body, I cannot tell: God knoweth;) such an one caught up to the third heaven. (2 Corinthians 12:2)

Though the apostle Paul uses the term "third heaven," this by no means implies there are two other levels of heaven where man will spend eternity; three levels of rewards for works performed in this life. The Bible does mention three heavens, but these include the atmospheric heaven, the celestial heaven, and the believer's heaven. There are scriptures to support this claim:

Deuteronomy 11:11 refers to the atmospheric heaven, where rain and clouds are formed:

But the land, whither ye go to possess it, is a land of hills and valleys, and drinketh water of the rain of heaven.

Psalm 147:8 also refers to this:

Who covereth the heaven with clouds, who prepareth rain for the earth, who maketh grass to grow upon the mountains.

Matthew 24:30 tells about Christ's return through this heaven:

And they shall see the Son of Man coming in the clouds of heaven with power and great glory.

Genesis 1:14 refers to the celestial heaven, where the sun, moon, and stars are:

And God said, Let there be lights in the firmament of the heaven to divide the day from the night; and let them be for signs, and for seasons, and for days, and years.

Isaiah 63:15 refers to the believer's heaven:

Look down from heaven, and behold from the habitation of thy holiness and thy glory: where is thy zeal and thy strength, the sounding of thy bowels and of thy mercies toward me? Are they restrained?

Psalm 102:19 also speaks of the believer's heaven:

For he hath looked down from the height of his sanctuary; from heaven did the Lord behold the earth.

Elijah went there in 2 Kings 2:11:

And it came to pass, as they still went on, and talked, that, behold, there appeared a chariot of fire, and horses of fire, and parted them both asunder; and Elijah went up by a whirlwind into heaven.

Paul, no doubt, was using words and expressions common to the people to whom he was writing. There is no verse in either the Bible or the *Book of Mormon* that states there are three destinations (or glories) awaiting man, each destination appropriate for the individual's works on earth. The Bible tells us plainly our destination will be either heaven or hell. Heaven is the final home for those who trust Christ as their Lord and Savior; hell is the destination of those who have put their trust in someone or something other than Christ and His sacrifice.

Many Mormons admit there is something that can bar them from the Mormon celestial kingdom: sin. Sin in their life at the time of death will force them to spend eternity in either of the lower two kingdoms, the telestial or terrestrial glories.

But according to Romans 3:23, "all have sinned and come short of the glory of God."

Sin does not force one to a lower glory, but rather prevents one's entrance into glory, period. God's plan of salvation is perfect. And nothing apart from it is acceptable.

Our hope is built on Jesus' cleansing blood:

If we confess our sins, he is faithful and just to forgive us our sins, and to cleanse us from all unrighteousness. (1 John 1:9)

27

Doesn't Acts 2:38 prove you must be baptized in order to be saved?

> Then Peter said unto them, Repent, and be baptized every one of you in the name of Jesus Christ for the remission of sins, and ye shall receive the gift of the Holy Ghost. (Acts 2:38)

The disagreement between Christian theology and Mormon theology stems from the use of the word *for* in this verse. Mormons claim Peter taught the act of baptism grants remission of sins. The Bible clearly states, however, that it is only the blood of Christ that cleanses from sin, not the water of baptism:

> In whom we have redemption through His blood, even the forgiveness of sins. (Colossians 1:14)

> But if we walk in the light, as he is in the light, we have fellowship one with another, and the blood of Jesus Christ his Son cleanseth us from all sin. (1 John 1:7)

The Greek text from which *for* is translated in Acts 2:38 uses the word *eis*. Pronounced "ace," the word in this context means "in view of" or "because of." You are not baptized to receive forgiveness, but rather *because* you have already been forgiven.

This same Greek word is translated "at" in Matthew 12:41:

> The men of Nineveh shall rise in judgment with this generation, and shall condemn it: because they repented *at* the preaching of Jonas. . . .

The Ninevites did not repent "to get" the preaching of Jonas, but rather "because of" the preaching of Jonas.

Another verse involved in this controversy is Mark 16:16:

> He that believeth and is baptized shall be saved; but he that believeth not shall be damned.

To fully support the Mormon idea that one must be baptized to be saved, the verse would have to read: "He that believeth not and is baptized not shall be damned." Since it does not read this way, we cannot assume it means this. There are many scriptures to support the idea that unbelief brings damnation, not a lack of baptism. The Word (Jesus, John 1:1) cleanses us, not water baptism.

Now ye are clean through the word which I have spoken unto you. (John 15:3)

That He might sanctify and cleanse it [the church] with the washing of water by the word. (Ephesians 5:26)

Not by works of righteousness which we have done, but according to his mercy he saved us, by the washing of regeneration, and the renewing of the Holy Ghost. (Titus 3:5)

28

Doesn't 1 Corinthians 15:29 prove the early church practiced baptism for the dead?

Else what shall they do which are baptized for the dead, if the dead rise not at all? why are they then baptized for the dead? (1 Corinthians 15:29)

Though there are many logical explanations concerning all the verses the Mormons use to substantiate baptizing for those who have died, none justifies the LDS belief that there will be a second chance for a person to be saved after death.

Paul uses the third person in 1 Corinthians 15:29, and appears to exclude himself from this practice: "Else what shall *they* do which are baptized. . . ?"

It would seem reasonable that if Paul actually performed the ritual himself, he would include himself when talking about it. Section 128:17 of *Doctrine and Covenants* says that baptism for the dead is the most "glorious of all subjects" belonging to the Everlasting Gospel. If this is true, Paul would likely have practiced it, and if he did would include himself when he spoke of it.

Luke 16:19 relates the story of Lazarus and the rich man. Personally, I believe Jesus was speaking of an actual event and not just telling one of His parables. The Lord never used names in His parables, but here He says there was a certain beggar named Lazarus. This makes it reasonable to believe there was a man by that name and that this story actually took place. The rich man died in his sins, and Abraham told the man there was no way he could escape his present, miserable state in the fiery flames. By this account, we know there was not, nor ever could be, a change in the rich man's situation. He had the opportunity during his lifetime to make his peace with God and he didn't do it.

Mormons also use 1 Peter 3:19 to support their claim that there is a chance for salvation after death:

> By which also he went and preached unto the spirits in prison.

They say this shows that Jesus Christ gave people who were dead another chance to accept the gospel. A closer study reveals this is not the case. The word "preached" in this verse is the Greek word *kerusso*, which, literally translated, means to hearken or proclaim. It does not mean to preach so as to convert. Jesus Christ went below to show himself to those who were disobedient, and to proclaim to them that had they been obedient, they would have tasted of His resurrection unto life. Instead, they will take part in the resurrection unto damnation (John 5:29).

Philippians 2:10–11 says every knee shall bow and every tongue confess that Jesus Christ is Lord. However, not everyone that bows will be able to call Him Savior. The people described in 1 Peter 3:19 are in the same place as the rich man of Luke 16:19. They are waiting, as sinners, to be judged at the great white throne of judgment (Revelation 20:11).

When the last explanation fails to convince the Mormon of his error, he will go to 1 Peter 4:6:

> For this cause was the gospel preached also to them that are dead.

The word "preached" in this passage is the Greek word *evangelizo*, which means "good tidings." However, the ones spoken of in this verse

The Salt Lake Temple

Though not the first temple built by the Church of Jesus Christ of Latter-day Saints, this building is certainly the most famous. In the temple, Mormons perform ritual baptisms for the dead as well as marriage ceremonies, which they believe are binding not only for this life, but also the next. For years the temple ceremony portrayed Christian pastors as hirelings of Satan who taught false doctrine. In April 1990, these offensive portions were removed even though the ceremony was supposedly given to Joseph Smith by revelation.

are not physically dead, but spiritually dead. When 1 Peter 4 is read in context, including verses four and five, we see that the people referred to in verse six are those described in verse four, and are still very much alive. The Bible teaches that there are two spiritual conditions: "dead in sin," and "dead to sin." The former refers to the sinner, the latter to the Christian. This particular passage is talking about those that are dead in sin.

Even if the people in verse six were physically dead, the account still would not support Mormon doctrine, because the passage reads in the past tense. To support the Mormon doctrine of the dead being given a second chance, it would have to read in the present tense: "For this cause *is* the gospel preached also to them that are dead."

Ironically, the *Book of Mormon* does not support the doctrine of an opportunity given to receive the gospel in the spirit world. In fact, the *Book of Mormon* does not even mention the practice of baptism for the dead, but rather shows clearly that salvation must be received before death:

> For that same spirit which doth possess your bodies at the time that ye go out of this life, that same spirit will have power to possess your body in that eternal world. For behold, if ye have procrastinated the day of your repentance even until death, behold, ye have become subjected to the spirit of the devil, and he doth seal you his; therefore, the Spirit of the Lord hath withdrawn from you, and hath no place in you, and the devil hath all power over you; and this is the final state of the wicked." (Alma 34:34–35).

Mormons argue that this refers only to those who know better and have rejected Mormonism, such as ex-Mormons or "Gentiles" who have done a great deal of study on Mormonism. This cannot be the case, for verse 32 says, "now is the time *for men* (in general) to prepare to meet God." It does not specify that the time is now for those who have understood fully and rejected.

In 2 Nephi 9:38 it says, "And, in fine, woe unto all those who die in their sins; for they shall return to God, and behold His face, and remain in their sins."

The Bible has a similar message—there is no chance for salvation after one dies in a sinful state:

> And as it is appointed unto men once to die, but after this the judgment. (Hebrews 9:27)

Since neither the Bible nor the *Book of Mormon* verifies the "second chance" doctrine, it is foolish for anyone—Mormon or otherwise—to live their life as though it were true. If you haven't accepted Jesus Christ as *your* personal Savior, *now* is the time.

> Behold, now is the accepted time; behold, now is the day of salvation. (2 Corinthians 6:2)

29

If there is no baptism for the dead, what about all those who died without having heard the Gospel?

This question is often asked by Mormons when their theory regarding the chance for salvation after death is refuted by the Scriptures. The question shows a lack of faith that God has the power to judge righteously. The Bible declares that He will judge with truth:

> Let the field be joyful, and all that is therein: then shall all the trees of the wood rejoice before the Lord: for he cometh, for he cometh to judge the earth: he shall judge the world with *righteousness*, and the people with His *truth*. (Psalm 96:12–13; italics added)

> The fear of the Lord is clean, enduring for ever: the judgments of the Lord are true and righteous altogether. (Psalm 19:9)

As a just and Holy God, the Lord will not allow anyone to go to hell who should not be there, nor will He deny entrance into His kingdom to anyone who should be there.

> The Lord is not slack concerning His promise, as some men count slackness; but is longsuffering toward us, not willing that any should perish, but that all should come to repentance. (2 Peter 3:9)

The Lord will make a way for the desiring heart to hear the Gospel, regardless of geographical barriers.

| 30 |

Why do you believe you need only faith in Jesus Christ to be saved when James 2:20 says faith without works is dead?

But wilt thou know, O vain man, that faith without works is dead? (James 2:20)

Mormonism maintains that though a person has faith in Jesus Christ, he must work to keep his salvation. Faith must be combined with works to gain exaltation into the Celestial Kingdom. Christians define salvation and exaltation as the same thing, while Mormonism makes *exaltation* a different kind of *salvation*.

Joseph Fielding Smith, the tenth President of the LDS church, stated:

Salvation is twofold: General—that which comes to all men irrespective of a belief (in this life) in Christ—and Individual—that which man merits through his own acts through life and by obedience to the laws and ordinances of the gospel. (*Doctrines of Salvation*, 1:134)

For the Mormon, individual salvation (exaltation) is the goal of life. To be exalted is to become a god over your own kingdom throughout eternity. Godhood to the Mormon is eternal life.

Joseph Smith taught:

Here then is eternal life—to know the only wise and true God; and you have got to learn how to be Gods yourselves, and to be kings and priests to God, the same as all Gods have done before you. (*Teachings of the Prophet Joseph Smith*, p. 346)

General salvation, or a mere resurrection to a lower heaven, is considered by many Mormons to be equal to damnation.

Faith and Works

Latter-day Saints use James 2:20 to support their belief that works must accompany faith if eternal life is to be gained. They don't realize

James is talking about the conduct of the Christian. Works are a *result* of faith, a life lived out of love for God. Many only see Christ through the life of a Christian. There must be something to see, some fruit of the life within us. If we profess a Holy Christ, we must live holy lives. Our daily actions must demonstrate the living God within. Works are a *result* of Christ's salvation given us, not something we do to *gain* the free gift of salvation.

If anyone had a reason to glory because of his works, it was Abraham, yet Romans 4:2 states:

> For if Abraham were justified by works, he hath whereof to glory; *but not before God.* (italics added)

This may seem to contradict James 2:21:

> Was not Abraham our father justified by works, when he had offered Isaac his son upon the altar?

It is important to remember what problem each of these men of God are addressing. Paul is attacking Phariseeism. The Pharisees were self-righteous and pointed to their outward appearance as a standard of righteousness. James addresses antinomianism, which literally means *against law*. Antinomians held that if a person's beliefs were correct, obeying a moral code was unnecessary.

To the Pharisees, Paul warned that works would profit little apart from a true faith. James tells the antinomians that a true faith should *produce* good works.

These two thoughts go hand in hand. Because Abraham had a true faith, his works naturally followed. He believed God, and it was accounted unto him for righteousness. His faith was turned into action.

We find in 1 Peter 1:5 that we are kept by the power of God through faith, not works:

> Who are kept by the power of God through faith unto salvation ready to be revealed in the last time.

And Ephesians 3:17 says:

> That Christ may dwell in your hearts by faith.

Joseph Fielding Smith maintains salvation is gained by following laws and ordinances. The apostle Paul makes it quite clear that following the law never got anyone saved. No one can keep the *whole* law! To fail in one point is to fail in all. It would be difficult to find a Mormon who could recite every one of the hundreds of laws connected with his religion, let alone keep them.

This is what Paul has to say about laws and ordinances:

> For he is our peace, who hath made both one, and hath broken down the middle wall of partition between us; Having abolished in his flesh the enmity, even the law of commandments contained in ordinances; for to make in himself of twain one new man, so making peace. (Ephesians 2:14–15)

> Blotting out the handwriting of ordinances that was against us, which was contrary to us, and took it out of the way, nailing it to his cross. (Colossians 2:14)

> Therefore by the deeds of the law shall no flesh be justified in his sight; for by the law is the *knowledge* of sin. (Romans 3:20; italics added)

The law has no power to save from sin, it merely points out man's imperfection, and his need for salvation.

Mormons insist that you must work for your exaltation. A mere faith in Christ will result in spending eternity in a lower form of heaven. Paul asks the questions:

> Are you so foolish? having begun in the Spirit, are ye now made perfect by the flesh? (Galatians 3:3)

> Where is boasting then? It is excluded. By what law? of works? Nay: but by the law of faith. (Romans 3:27)

You began in faith. Do you think you will be exalted because of your works? Don't be foolish. Works bring boasting. The law of faith excludes it.

Because Christians accept the biblical fact that salvation comes by faith, Mormons think the Christian believes all he has to do is say he believes and that's all there is to it—just go and have a good time; everything is taken care of. Of course this is not the case, because the Lord says in John 14:15, "If ye love me, keep my commandments."

What are His commandments?

> And this is his commandment, That we should believe on the

name of his Son Jesus Christ, and love one another, as he gave us commandment. (1 John 3:23)

The true Christian keeps the commandments of the Lord, not to earn or keep his salvation, but because he loves the Lord who first loved him. The Christian also loves and cares for the lost, and for this reason will seek to live a holy life. He will refrain from doing anything that might hinder another from coming to Christ. Because we are no longer under the law does not mean that we continue in sin.

What then? shall we sin, because we are not under the law, but under grace? God forbid. (Romans 6:15)

The Mormon's salvation can be likened to the father who says to his son, "Son, if you mow the lawn tomorrow I will take you to the park."

The Christian's salvation can be likened to the father who says to his son, "Son, tomorrow I am going to take you the park." Out of love and appreciation for his father, the son mows the lawn without being asked. He is not doing it to gain a trip to the park, because that was already promised, and he believes his father will take him. Love and appreciation for what his heavenly Father has done for him results in a Christian's performance of good works.

Ephesians 2:8–9 sums it up:

For by grace are ye saved through faith; and that not of yourselves: it is the gift of God: Not of works, lest any man should boast.

There is no logical way the Mormon definitions of the word salvation can fit into these passages. For instance, if Paul were talking about general salvation or resurrection, substituting the word saved with resurrected, the passage would read: "For by grace are ye *resurrected* through faith."

The Mormons would not accept this explanation since faith is not a requirement for resurrection. If Paul were talking about exaltation or Godhood in Ephesians 2:8–9, the passage might read: "For by grace are ye *exalted* through faith; and that not of yourselves; it is the gift of God: *not of works* [?] lest any man should boast."

Grace is bestowed upon no one until they put their faith in Christ. The fact that Jesus died on the cross does not, in and of itself, save. His death is not effectual to the individual until he believes and accepts

Christ's substitutional death for himself. Jesus was without sin; He did not pay the penalty for His own sin, which is death, but the penalty of our sins. Romans 3:23 says:

> All have sinned and come short of the glory of God.

Man's condition made the sacrifice necessary, and Christ's death is enough reason for man to give control of his life to Christ and trust Him fully for salvation.
Matthew 7:21 says:

> Not every one that saith unto me, Lord, Lord, shall enter into the kingdom of heaven; but he that doeth the will of my Father which is in heaven.

What is the will of the Father?

> And this is the will of him that sent me, that every one which seeth the Son, and *believeth* on him, may have everlasting life: and I will raise him up at the last day. (John 6:40; italics added)

Mormons will argue that we must work out our salvation as stated in Philippians 2:12:

> Work out your own salvation with fear and trembling.

Notice it does not say *work for* your salvation, but *work out* your salvation. Undoubtedly, there is work to do in the Christian walk. It takes effort to set time aside to study the Word of God and to spend time in prayer and intercession. It takes discipline to rebuke negative and evil thoughts the devil might throw at us. Every Christian has his own set of problems and difficulties with which he must learn to cope and work out to maintain his testimony. But in spite of what we may face, it is only through faith in the true and living God that these things can be accomplished!

$$\boxed{31}$$

Who do you think the angel is in Revelation 14:6 if it isn't Moroni?

The Bible does not give any indication as to who the angel is in Revelation 14:6:

> And I saw another angel fly in the midst of heaven, having the everlasting gospel to preach unto them that dwell on the earth, and to every nation, and kindred, and tongue, and people.

One thing is clear, however. The angel cannot possibly be the angel Moroni, nor can the everlasting gospel be the *Book of Mormon*, as supposed by the LDS church.

Reading the first fourteen chapters of the book of Revelation, one can readily see that the event described in verse six must still come to pass. It is described as a futuristic event.

If Mormons insist on abusing the Scriptures by saying Revelation 14:6 is referring to Moroni and the *Book of Mormon*, they must also identify the other angels who are described in the book of Revelation; for surely if verse six has taken place, the others have also, since they are in chronological order.

In light of Mormon history, the angel could be Nephi and not Moroni. While the Mormon church validates Joseph Smith's account of his seeing an angel named Moroni in 1838, just two years before Smith died, he is quoted as saying he saw an angel named Nephi. The *Book of Mormon* describes Moroni as the son of Mormon, and Nephi as the son of Lehi, a completely different character. On April 15, 1842, the Mormon publication *Times and Seasons*, 3:753, quoted Smith as saying:

> While I was thus in the act of calling upon God I discovered a light appearing in the room which continued to increase until the room was lighter than at noon-day, when immediately a personage appeared at my bedside standing in the air for his feet did not touch the floor . . . He called me by name, and said unto me that he was

a messenger sent from the presence of God to me, and that his name was Nephi.

This account also appears in the 1851 edition of the *Pearl of Great Price*.

32

Why do you criticize the Mormon church for the doctrine of polygamy when a number of great men in the Bible practiced it also?

While it is true that many great men of the Bible did have more than one wife, it appears God's position on the matter was one of toleration rather than commandment.

We find that monogamy was God's norm as early as Genesis 2:24:

> Therefore shall a man leave his father and his mother, and shall cleave unto his wife: and they shall be one flesh.

Matthew 19:5 and Mark 10:7–8 express the same thought. The singular *wife* is used in every case, never *wives*.

Deuteronomy 17:17 charges specifically that kings were not to multiply wives unto themselves, and Leviticus 21:13–14 states that the high priest was to marry a virgin.

While we cannot deny that polygamy did take place in Old Testament Israel, we find no example of it in the New Testament church. And because Jesus quotes Genesis 2:24 in both Matthew 19:5 and Mark 10:7, it appears that God had not changed His position on the matter.

Monogamy was taught by the apostle Paul in 1 Corinthians 7:2:

> Let every man have his own wife, and let every woman have her own husband.

In 1 Timothy 3:2 we are directly charged that officers in the Church must not have more than one wife:

A bishop then must be blameless, the husband of one wife.

Much of the criticism brought upon the Mormon church for their views on polygamy probably stems more from their vacillation on the subject. While polygamy is not to be practiced today, in the past it was a specific command in Mormonism that never was to have ended. Despite many quotes from early Mormon leaders who insist polygamy was a significant part of the religion that could not be given up, the practice was officially abolished in 1890 with the writing of *The Manifesto*.

One of the ways Mormon leaders justified the practice of having plural wives was by teaching that God the Father and Jesus Christ were practicing polygamists. Said Mormon Apostle Orson Pratt:

> We have now clearly shown that God the Father had a plurality of wives, one or more being in eternity, by whom He begat our spirits as well as the spirit of Jesus His First Born, and another being upon the earth by whom He begat the tabernacle of Jesus, as his only Begotten in this world. (*The Seer*, p. 172)

In this statement Pratt confirms the Mormon tenet that God was married for a time to Mary. As a glorified human being, Mormonism teaches that through a physical relationship Mary conceived the child Jesus. This is clearly defined by Bruce McConkie in his book, *Mormon Doctrine*, p. 547:

> Christ was begotten by an Immortal Father *in the same way* mortal men are begotten by mortal fathers.

In the same book McConkie declares,

> [Jesus] was born in the same personal, real, and literal sense that any mortal son is born to a mortal father. There is nothing figurative about his paternity; he was begotten, conceived and born in the normal and natural course of events, for he is the Son of God, and that designation means what it says (p. 742).

What really boggles the mind is that McConkie insists at the same time that he believes in the Virgin Birth:

> Modernistic teachings denying the virgin birth are utterly and completely apostate and false (p. 822).

How can this Mormon leader believe Jesus was begotten like any other mortal and still believe in the virgin birth? He claims that because Mary had sexual relations with an *immortal* man, she was still a virgin. Virginity is defined as never having sexual relations with another human. McConkie also states in his book,

> Our Lord is the only mortal person ever born to a virgin, because he is the only person who ever had an immortal Father (p. 822).

The fact that Mormonism teaches we are all the literal offspring of the Heavenly Father and one of His heavenly wives, we must conclude that Mary was also one of His literal daughters created first in the "pre-existence." Carried to its only logical (?) conclusion, Mormons must ad-

Orson Pratt
In November 1853, Orson Pratt made it quite clear that Mormon doctrine taught both God the Father and Jesus Christ were practicing polygamists.

mit that they believe Jesus was conceived through an incestuous relationship between their Heavenly Father and one of His literal children. It is no wonder this doctrine is highly offensive to Bible-believing Christians.

As we have stated before, there are plenty of references that prove polygamy was never meant to end among the Mormons. George Q. Cannon, who served in the First Presidency under Brigham Young, stated on July 20, 1879:

> If plural marriage be divine, as the Latter-day Saints say it is, no power on earth can suppress it, unless you crush and destroy the entire people. (*Journal of Discourses*, 20:276)

In 1869 Wilford Woodruff stated,

> If we were to do away with polygamy, it would only be one feather in the bird, one ordinance in the Church and kingdom. Do away with that, then we must do away with Prophets and Apostles, with

blessings which Abraham obtained, you will be polygamists at least in your faith, or you will come short of enjoying the salvation and the glory which Abraham has obtained. This is as true as that God lives. You who wish that there were no such thing in existence, if you have in your hearts to say : " We will pass along in the Church without obeying or submitting to it in our faith or believing this order, because, for aught that we know, this community may be broken up yet, and we may have lucrative offices offered to us; we will not, therefore, be polygamists lest we should fail in obtaining some earthly honor, character and office, etc,"— the man that has that in his heart, and will continue to persist in pursuing that policy, will come short of dwelling in the presence of the Father and the Son, in celestial glory. <u>The only men who become Gods, even the Sons of God, are those who enter into polygamy.</u> Others attain unto a glory and may even be permitted to come into the presence of the Father and the Son; but they cannot reign as kings in glory, because they had blessings offered unto them, and they refused to accept them.

The Lord gave a revelation through Joseph Smith, His servant; and we have believed and practiced it. Now, then, it is said that this must be done away before we are permitted to receive our place as a State in the Union It may be, or it may not be. One of the twin relics—slavery— they say, is abolished. I do not, however, wish to speak about this ; but if slavery and oppression and iron-handed cruelty are not more felt by the blacks to-day than before, I am glad of it. My heart is pained for that unfortunate race of men. One twin relic having been strangled, the other, they say, must next be destroyed. It is they and God for it,

and you will all find that out. It is not Brigham Young, Heber C. Kimball and Daniel H. Wells and the Elders of Israel they are fighting against; but it is the Lord Almighty. What is the Lord going to do ? He is going to do just as he pleases, and the world cannot help themselves.

I heard the revelation on polygamy, and I believed it with all my heart, and I know it is from God— I know that he revealed it from heaven; I know that it is true, and understand the bearings of it and why it is. " Do you think that we shall ever be admitted as a State into the Union without denying the principle of polygamy ?" If we are not admitted until then, we shall never be admitted. These things will be just as the Lord will. Let us live to take just what he sends to us, and when our enemies rise up against us, we will meet them as we can, and exercise faith and pray for wisdom and power more than they have, and contend continually for the right. Go along, my children, saith the Lord, do all you can, and remember that your blessings come through your faith. Be faithful and cut the corners of your enemies where you can—get the advantage of them by faith and good works, take care of yourselves, and they will destroy themselves. Be what you should be, live as you should, and all will be well.

Who knows but the time will come when the inquiry will be made in Washington, by the President, by the Congressmen : " Are things any worse in Utah than in Washington : than they are in New York ? or in any State of the Union ? are they more unvirtuous, are they more disloyal to the Government ? But then there is polygamy." That has nothing in the least to do with our being loyal or disloyal, one way or the other. But is not the practice of

---

In 1866 Brigham Young claimed the only men who become gods, even the Sons of God, are those who enter into polygamy (Journal of Discourses, 2:269).

SEC. CX.]   APPENDIX.   331

that is, keeping yourselves wholly for each other, and
from all others, during your lives." And when they
have answered "Yes," he shall pronounce them "husband and wife," in the name of the Lord Jesus Christ
and by virtue of the laws of the country and authority
vested in him : "May God add his blessings, and
keep you to fulfil your covenants from henceforth and
for ever. Amen."

3. The clerk of every church should keep a record of
all marriages solemnized in his branch.

4. All legal contracts of marriage made before a person is baptized into this church should be held sacred
and fulfilled. Inasmuch as this church of Christ has
been reproached with the crime of fornication, and
polygamy ; we declare that we believe that one man
should have one wife ; and one woman but one husband, except in case of death, when either is at liberty
to marry again. It is not right to persuade a woman
to be baptized contrary to the will of her husband ;
neither is it lawful to influence her to leave her husband. All children are bound by law to obey their
parents ; and to influence them to embrace any religious faith, or be baptized, or leave their parents without their consent, is unlawful and unjust. We believe
that husbands, parents, and masters, who exercise control over their wives, children, and servants, and pre-
vent them from embracing the truth, will have to
answer for that sin.

SECTION CX.

OF GOVERNMENTS AND LAWS IN GENERAL.

That our belief with regard to earthly governments and
laws in general may not be misinterpreted nor misun-
derstood, we have thought proper to present at the close
of this volume our opinion concerning the same.

1. We believe that governments were instituted of
God for the benefit of man, and that he holds men ac-

That same year, the British edition of Doctrine and Covenants *denied the
doctrine of plural marriage and stated polygamy was a "crime of fornication"*
(Doctrine and Covenants, *Liverpool, England, 1866. Sec. CIX:4*).

revelation and the gifts and graces of the Gospel, and finally give up our religion altogether and turn sectarians and do as the world does, then all would be right. (*Journal of Discourses*, v.13:166)

Mr. Woodruff had quite a turn around, for as the fourth president of the Mormon church, it was he who signed the *Manifesto* that abolished polygamy twenty-one years later.

According to the teachings of early Mormonism, polygamy, or celestial marriage, was essential if one wished to attain Godhood. Brigham Young made this very clear in 1866 when he said,

> The only men who become Gods, even the Sons of God, are those who enter into polygamy. (*Journal of Discourses*, 11:269)

The deceitfulness and inconsistency of the Mormon leadership at this time is evident in the fact that while polygamy was being taught as a must for Godhood, it was being denied in their sacred *Doctrine and Covenants*. The 1866 edition of the *Doctrine and Covenants* printed in Liverpool, England, stated:

> Inasmuch as this church of Christ has been reproached with the crime of fornication and polygamy; we declare that one man should have one wife; and one woman but one husband, except in case of death, when either is at liberty to marry again. (Sec. CIX:4)

Imagine the surprise of the new immigrants to Utah when they discovered the book they had read in Europe did not reflect the doctrine being taught in the Salt Lake Valley!

While Brigham Young and his contemporaries may have believed polygamy was essential to Godhood, to practice it today would result in excommunication. *Mormon Doctrine*, p. 549, reads:

> All who pretend or assume to engage in plural marriage in this day, when the one holding the keys has withdrawn the power by which they are performed, are guilty of gross wickedness.

While Mormons are not to practice plural marriage in this day and age, Mormon doctrine maintains it will be practiced when Jesus returns:

> Obviously the holy practice will commence again after the Second Coming of the Son of Man and the ushering in of the millennium. (*Mormon Doctrine*, p. 578)

Some have argued that polygamy was essential during its time in Mormon history because there were more Mormon women than Mormon men. This hypothesis is rejected by Mormon Apostle John Widtsoe, who wrote in his book, *Evidences and Reconciliations*, pp. 390–391:

> The most common of these conjectures is that the Church, through plural marriage, sought to provide husbands for its large surplus of female members. The implied assumption in this theory, that there have been more female than male members in the Church, is not supported by existing evidence. On the contrary, there seem always to have been more males than females in the Church . . . The United States census records from 1850 to 1940 and all available Church records, uniformly show a preponderance of males in Utah, and in the Church . . . The theory that plural marriage was a consequence of a surplus of female members fails from lack of evidence.

33

Do you actually believe God is going to punish His children with a literal hell of fire and flames?

To answer this we must first define the Bible's meaning of *God's children*. Many believe that because we are God's human creation we are automatically His children. This is contrary to Bible teaching. Each of us is a creation of God; however, to become a child of God we must be born into His family by the Spirit.

John 1:12 states that the "power" or authority to become sons of God comes by receiving Him as Savior:

> But as many as received him, to *them* gave he power to become the sons of God, even to them that believe on his name. (John 1:12)

Jesus told Nicodemus that this birth into God's family could only come about by way of a spiritual birth, not physical. It is described as being born again or the second birth. Those who have been born again spiritually are the rightful children and heirs of God. None who have been born into God's family, by faith in His name, will be punished in a hell of literal fire and flames.

However, those who have spurned God's sacrifice and refused the love gift of His Son, unfortunately, will spend eternity in endless torment, according to the Scriptures.

Revelation 20:15 says:

> And whosoever was not found written in the book of life was cast into the lake of fire.

When the Lord appeared to Moses in the burning bush (Exodus 3:2), the words used to describe the bush that was not consumed with the fire are the same used when describing the lost in Revelation 20:15. Those who reject the free gift of life offered by Jesus Christ will spend eternity burning but will not be consumed.

The *Book of Mormon* also has many things to say concerning a literal hell of fire and flames:

> And according to the power of justice, for justice cannot be denied, ye must go away into that lake of fire and brimstone, whose flames are unquenchable, and whose smoke ascendeth up forever and ever, which lake of fire and brimstone is endless torment. (Jacob 6:10)

> And finally, all ye that will persist in your wickedness, I say unto you that these are they who shall be hewn down and cast into the fire except they speedily repent. (Alma 5:56)

> And they who are filthy shall be filthy still; wherefore, they who are filthy are the devil and his angels; and they shall go away into everlasting fire, prepared for them; and their torment is as a lake of fire and brimstone, whose flame ascendeth up forever and ever and has no end. (2 Nephi 9:16)

It may be argued that because 2 Nephi 9:16 says "is *as* a lake of fire" it implies figurative speech. However, the original 1830 edition clears up any misinterpretation. The first *Book of Mormon* does not use the word "as" in this verse. It was added later. One might ask, if the first edition had God's seal of approval, which Mormons claim it did, why all the later corrections?

The subject of eternal punishment is not one of the most popular topics of discussion (especially among those who fear they are destined for it), but it must not be overlooked. The Mormon has no excuse for rejecting this teaching, because the *Book of Mormon* is explicit about the consequences awaiting anyone who rejects the One who created him. For the Mormon to believe there is no hell of fire and flames is for him to reject the book he claims to be sacred Scripture.

The *Book of Mormon* also has something to say concerning those who claim there is no hell:

> And others will he [Satan] pacify, and lull them away into carnal security, that they will say: All is well in Zion; yea, Zion prospereth, all is well—and thus the devil cheateth their souls, and leadeth them away carefully down to hell.

> And behold, others will be flattereth away, and telleth them there is no hell; and he saith unto them: I am no devil, for there is none—and thus he whispereth in their ears, until he grasps them with his awful chains, from whence there is no deliverance. (2 Nephi 28:21–22)

What makes these verses so significant is that while it is the devil who tells people there is no hell, Mormon Apostle John Widtsoe, in his book, *Joseph Smith—Seeker After Truth*, p. 178, says the same thing:

> In the Church of Jesus Christ of Latter-day Saints there is no hell. All will find a measure of salvation . . . The gospel of Jesus Christ has no hell in the old proverbial sense.

34

Have you prayed concerning the truthfulness of the Book of Mormon?

This question is probably the most common of all questions Mormons ask. Many times it is the one asked after the Mormon's testimony has already been refuted by the Scriptures. The Mormon missionary is, in essence, saying: "Forget the facts and just pray about it."

But should we pray whether or not it is right to commit murder or adultery? Should we pray about whether it is okay to hate our brother? Of course not. The Bible speaks clearly concerning these subjects. Prayer is not necessary to know God's will in these areas. It has already been revealed.

And God has already spoken concerning the *Book of Mormon*. The Christian has no reason to pray about its authenticity.

Galatians 1:8 says:

> But though we, or an angel from heaven, preach any other gospel unto you than that which we have preached unto you, let him be accursed.

Paul repeats himself in verse 9, in an effort to get the point across clearly:

> As we said before, so say I now again, if any man preach any other gospel unto you than that ye have received, let him be accursed.

The Mormon will argue that the *Book of Mormon* is not another gospel but another testament of Christ. If this is true, why do Mormons worship a god so entirely different than that of the Bible?

Their god is a god of flesh and bones (*Doctrine and Covenants*, 130:22), whereas the God of the Bible is an invisible Spirit (John 4:24, Hebrews 11:27). Their god was once a man (*Teachings of the Prophet Joseph Smith*, p. 345), while the God of the Bible was always God from everlasting to everlasting (Psalm 90:2).

Mormon dogma says man is saved "by grace . . . after all we can do" (2 Nephi 25:23); the gospel of the Bible says we are saved by grace because of the righteousness of Christ.

In light of what we have researched and quoted in previous chapters of this book, the gospel of Mormonism is far different from the Gospel of the Bible.

When set in the proper context, the same scriptures that Mormons believe support their beliefs crush the very foundation of their church.

As Christians we are to test the spirits, not pray over them. We are told in 1 John 4:1:

> Beloved, believe not every spirit, but try the spirits whether they are of God: because many false prophets are gone out into the world.

The claims of Mormonism do not withstand investigation when examined under the searchlight of the Bible. And not only does the Bible destroy their claims of "truthfulness"; their own history of contradictions and censorship proves to the thinking person that Mormonism cannot be of God.

If Mormonism cannot pass the test of 1 John 4:1, its "truthfulness" should not be pursued any longer.

| 35 |

Why don't you think the Book of Mormon is inspired by God?

Events leading up to the printing of the *Book of Mormon* should cause the Bible-believing Christian to doubt its divine inspiration. We are commanded to try the spirits and prove all things by the authority of the Scriptures.

If Joseph Smith relied upon the Scriptures to determine truth, he should have been wary of the beings he claims to have seen in the woods. The fact that he said he saw both God the Father and Jesus should bring suspicion enough in light of John 1:18:

No man hath seen God at any time.

Even Joseph Smith claimed no one could see God without the Holy Priesthood, and Mormon history shows us Smith had no such Priesthood in 1820 when this vision supposedly took place. In fact, he didn't receive the priesthood until nine years later.

The beings in Smith's vision claimed all the churches at that time were wrong and all their doctrines corrupt. If that were true, why does Mormonism have some doctrines in common with Christian denominations? Certainly if *all* the doctrines of the Christian churches were wrong, Mormonism should not have any doctrine in common with biblical Christianity.

Later Smith was visited by an angel who was so bright his "room

The original *Book of Mormon*

The title page of the original 1830 edition of the Book of Mormon *states Smith was the author. Later editions were changed to claim he was the translator. Only 5,000 copies were printed in 1830.*

was lighter than at noon day." Immediately 2 Corinthians 11:14 comes to mind:

> And no marvel, for Satan himself is transformed into an angel of light.

Instead of confirming the truthfulness of God's Word, the angel told him of plates that contain the "fullness of the everlasting gospel." Another gospel?

> But though we, or an angel from heaven, preach any other gospel unto you than that which we have preached unto you, let him be accursed. (Galatians 1:8–9)

A true Christian, seeing what Smith saw, would trust Galatians 1:8–9, knowing there is no other gospel. Paul said we should trust in what we have already received. Though the Mormon may seek to justify his scriptures, the fact remains, Mormonism is full of doctrine not found in the Bible.

The contents of the *Book of Mormon* would raise doubts in the mind and heart of anyone who held the Bible dear. An example of its poor logic is found in the book of Ether. God tells the brother of Jared to build barges that are so airtight the inhabitants inside can't breathe. When the brother of Jared complains about the problem, he is told to put a hole in the top and bottom of the boat! Apparently not knowing whether or not water will come into the hole in the bottom of the boat, the Mormon god tells him that *if* the water comes in he should plug the hole back up (Ether 2:20).

Also in the book of Ether, we find the fight to the death between Coriantumr and Shiz. Coriantumr wins by cutting off the head of Shiz. But strangely, even without his head:

> Shiz raised upon his hands and fell; and after he had struggled for breath, he died. (Ether 15:31)

Plagiarism

Neither can we overlook all the plagiarized Bible stories in the *Book of Mormon*.

In 1 Nephi 4:18–19, we see shades of David and Goliath, only in this story Nephi (the David figure) takes off Laban's head with his own sword. Nephi also plays Samson in 1 Nephi 7:17–18.

Unlike the story of Adam and Eve, Lehi has a dream in which one was supposed to partake of the tree where the "fruit was desirable to make one happy" (1 Nephi 8).

In 1 Nephi 16:20, the "sons of Ishmael" are murmuring in the wilderness much like the children of Israel in the book of Exodus. Also, the book of Mosiah tells of taskmasters (24:9), as in the book of Exodus.

Similar to Saul's conversion on the Damascus road is the conversion of Alma, who goes around "seeking to destroy the church of God." In Mosiah 27, an angel of the Lord appears, the men fall to the earth, and—much like the story of Saul in the book of Acts—don't understand the words spoken to them. Alma is told to rise and is asked, "Why persecutest thou the church of God?" Like Paul, Alma gives an account of his conversion in Alma 36.

The counterparts to the Bible's Paul and Silas are Alma and Amulek of the *Book of Mormon* (Alma 8:31–32).

Similar to the story in Daniel, Alma 10:2 tells of handwriting on the wall "written by the finger of God."

As Jesus was questioned by the lawyers, Alma is questioned in Alma 10:14–17.

Alma 14:14–27 records an earthquake similar to the one we read of in Acts 16:26. It shakes down the walls freeing not Paul, but Alma.

So many parallels raise suspicion in anyone knowledgeable in the Bible.

The *Book of Mormon* includes literally hundreds of verses copied almost word for word from the King James Version. Even the added italicized words were copied, words not included in the original languages that had been added by the translators to make the text easier to understand in English.

It also quotes the apostle Paul. But it is odd that he is often quoted before he existed or before he became a Christian. For instance, Alma 58:40 uses the phrase "Stand fast in that liberty wherewith God hath made them free." We recognize this phrase from Galatians 5:1. However, the *Book of Mormon* dates it to the year 63 B.C., long before Paul was even born!

A Not-So-Perfect Translation

If the *Book of Mormon* is indeed an inspired book, why has the LDS leadership changed it so often? The Mormon who claims his *Book of*

Mormon is an exact copy of the one God gave Joseph Smith is speaking from ignorance. The truth is, it has thousands of changes not included in its original 1830 printing. Mormons might defend this by pointing to the many Bible translations available today, while as Christians we know the original manuscripts were, in fact, "God-breathed" and infallible, a translation from those manuscripts can, in some areas, be improved. The *Book of Mormon*, on the other hand, was "translated by the gift and power of God" and can have no errors.

In his book, *An Address to All Believers in Christ*, David Whitmer, one of the three witnesses listed in every *Book of Mormon*, states that Smith used a "Seer Stone" during his translation of the gold plates. This seer stone was a chocolate-colored, egg-shaped rock Smith claimed had mystical powers. David Whitmer describes the manner in which Smith translated the plates:

> I will now give you a description of the manner in which the *Book of Mormon* was translated. Joseph Smith would put the Seer Stone into a hat, and put his face in the hat, drawing it closely around his face to exclude the light; and in the darkness the spiritual light would shine. A piece of something resembling parchment would appear, and on that appeared the writing. One character at a time would appear, and under it was the interpretation in English. Brother Joseph would read off the English to Oliver Cowdery, who was his principal [sic] scribe, and when it was written down and repeated to Brother Joseph to see if it was correct, then it would disappear, and another character with the interpretation would appear. Thus the *Book of Mormon* was translated by the gift and power of God, and not by any power of man (p. 12).

From this account we see that Smith wasn't even looking at the plates at the time of translation. In fact, Smith's brother William gives this account about the translation of the plates:

> The manner in which this was done was by looking into the Urim and Thummim, which was placed in a hat to exclude the light, (the plates lying nearby covered up), and reading off the translation which appeared in the stone by the power of God. (*A New Witness for Christ in America*, 2:417)

It makes one wonder why Smith went to the trouble of digging up these mysterious plates when he apparently didn't need to look at them.

Oliver B. Huntington wrote in his journal on Saturday, February 28, 1881:

> Heard Joseph F. Smith [Mormonism's sixth President] describe the manner of translating the *Book of Mormon* by Joseph Smith, the prophet and Seer, which was as follows as near as I can recollect the substance of his description. Joseph did not render the writing on the Gold plates into the English language in his own style of language as many people believe, but every word and every letter was given to him by the gift and power of God . . . The Lord caused each word spelled as it is in the book to appear on the stones in short sentences or words and when Joseph had uttered the sentence or word before him and the scribe had written it properly, that sentence would disappear and another appear. And if there was a word wrongly written or even a letter incorrect the writing on the stones would remain there.

If this method were used, there is absolutely *no* margin for error. The subsequent changes might be charged to mistakes by the printer, but the manuscript given to the printer does not support the later changes.

The quotes also show that Joseph Smith used occultic practices to bring about this "sacred" record. Seer stones or peep stones were quite common among those who were involved in folk magic and there is little question that Joseph Smith, as well as his parents, were actively involved in folk magic.

LDS historian D. Michael Quinn admits in his book *Early Mormonism and the Magic World View*:

> Occult beliefs and magic practices were part of early America's heritage and experience. Early Americans who did not share the magic world view condemned such beliefs and practices as irrational and anti-religious, but intelligent and religious Americans who perceived reality from a magic view regarded such beliefs and practices as both rational and religious. Within this latter category of religious and intelligent people were Joseph Smith, members of his family, the witnesses to the *Book of Mormon*, several of the first apostles in the LDS church, as well as other church authorities and early Mormons who manifested various beliefs and practices of the magic world view (pp. 225-226).

Joseph Smith himself claimed the *Book of Mormon* was "the most correct of any book on earth" (*History of the Church*, 4:461). Yet, it can be easily proven that many changes were made long after the original 1830 edition. For example, in the 1908 edition the phrase "or out of the waters of baptism" was still not a part of 1 Nephi 20:1.

In 1981 still more changes were made to the "most correct of any book on earth." Once 2 Nephi 30:6 taught that the Lamanites (persons of dark skin) would turn white and delightsome when they embraced the Mormon doctrine. Because this was not happening, the portion referring to Lamanites turning white was changed to read they would turn "pure."

Doctrinal Discrepancies With Mormonism

Close examination of the *Book of Mormon* makes one wonder if Joseph Smith remembered what he wrote. In the *Doctrine and Covenants* he says,

> The idea that the Father and the Son dwell in a man's heart is an old sectarian notion, and is false. (130:3)

Yet, earlier in Alma 34:36 he wrote:

> And this I know, because the Lord hath said he dwelleth not in unholy temples, but in the hearts of the righteous doth he dwell.

He also contradicted the *Book of Mormon* by saying,

> We have imagined and supposed that God was God from all eternity. I will refute that idea, and take away the veil, so that you may see. (*Teachings of the Prophet Joseph Smith*, p. 345)

The idea he refuted is found in Moroni 8:18, which reads:

> For I know that God is not a partial God, neither a changeable being; but he is unchangeable, from all eternity to all eternity.

According to 2 Nephi 24:13–14, one would think the last thing Mormons would want is to exalt themselves to Godhood. The passage is copied from Isaiah 14:13–15:

> For thou hast said in thine heart: I will ascend into heaven, I will exalt my throne above the stars of God . . . Yet thou shalt be brought down to hell, to the sides of the pit.

In spite of this warning, First Counselor Charles Penrose stated:

> Mormonism does not tend to debase God to the level of man, but to exalt man to the perfection of God. (*Gospel Through the Ages*, p. 107)

Some Mormons have used Matthew 18:16 to support the authenticity of the *Book of Mormon*:

> In the mouth of two or three witnesses every word may be established.

They contend this scripture justifies the existence of the *Book of Mormon* since they claim it is "another testament" of Christ, a second witness. However, the Old and New Testaments consistently refer to multiple witnesses when charges are brought against a person who has sinned. Never do the Scriptures give any indication that another book is necessary to testify of Christ and His divinity. The Mormon church has clearly taken this, and other similar passages, out of context to buttress their claim.

There are many serious problems in the *Book of Mormon* and its history that LDS church leaders are afraid to tackle. The changes alone are warning enough that something is amiss. If the Mormon leadership does not reverence its contents, why should anyone else?

Why don't you believe Joseph Smith was a true prophet of God?

Of all the tests that can be applied to Mormonism in an effort to prove whether it is from God or not, the test to determine the authority of its founder should be the most obvious. As Joseph Fielding Smith stated:

> He [Joseph Smith] was either a prophet of God, divinely called, properly appointed and commissioned, or he was one of the biggest

frauds the world has ever seen, there is no middle ground. (*Doctrines of Salvation*, 1:188)

The Bible presents several tests for prophets. Deuteronomy 18:21 asks how one can know "the word which the Lord hath not spoken." The answer is given in verse 22:

When a prophet speaketh in the name of the Lord, if the thing follow not, nor come to pass, that is the thing which the Lord hath not spoken, but the prophet hath spoken it presumptuously: thou shalt not be afraid of him.

Deuteronomy 18:20 gives the penalty for a prophet who presumes to speak in the name of the Lord, or who speaks in the name of other gods: death.

Other scriptures that warn of false prophets and show God's judgment of them are Deuteronomy 13:1–5 and Jeremiah 23:31–32.

False Prophecies

Joseph Smith is responsible for a long list of false prophecies. We will discuss a few of them briefly.

Smith earned the title of false prophet very early. In the beginning of his new movement, he gave a false prophecy concerning the sale of the copyright of the *Book of Mormon* in Canada. Though Smith claimed God had said it would be sold, the two men sent to perform the task came back having failed to do so (David Whitmer, *An Address to All Believers in Christ*, p. 31).

Richard Lloyd Anderson, professor of ancient scripture at Brigham Young University, claims Whitmer was in error concerning this revelation and quotes Hyrum Page, one of the eight witness to the *Book of Mormon*, as saying that Smith ordered them to go to Kingston, not Toronto (*A Sure Foundation*, p. 42) as stated by Whitmer. Because of this apparent discrepancy, Anderson appears to discount the entire record.

Nevertheless, Mormon historian B. H. Roberts, who admits Whitmer's representation of some of the facts could be flawed, writes, "his testimony may not be set aside" (*Comprehensive History of the Church*, 1:165).

Today's LDS apologists hold to Hyrum Page's account because it the day. While this was progressing great numbers were being baptized in the font.

Those who wish for further information concerning the scenes of the Sabbath in Nauvoo, or any other day in the week would do well to "come and see."   W. WOODRUFF.

HISTORY OF JOSEPH SMITH.
(Continued.)

While I was thus in the act of calling upon God I discovered a light appearing in the room which continued to increase until the room was lighter than at noonday, when immediately a personage appeared at my bedside standing in the air for his feet did not touch the floor. He had on a loose robe of most exquisite whiteness. It was a whiteness beyond anything earthly I had ever seen; nor do I believe that any earthly thing could be made to appear so exceedingly white and brilliant, his hands were naked and his arms also a little above the wrist. So also were his feet naked, as were his legs a little above the ankles. His head and neck were also bare. I could discover that he had no other clothing on but this robe, as it was open so that I could see into his bosom. Not only was his robe exceedingly white but his whole person was glorious beyond description, and his countenance truly like lightning. The room was exceedingly light, but not so very bright as immediately around his person. When I first looked upon him I was afraid, but the fear soon left me. He called me by name, and said unto me that he was a messenger sent from the presence of God to me, and that his name was Nephi. That God had a work for me to do, and that my name should be had for good and evil, among all nations, kindreds, and tongues; or that it should be both good and evil spoken of among all people. He said there was a book deposited written upon gold plates, giving an account of the former inhabitants of this continent, and the source from whence they sprang. He also said that the fullness of the everlasting gospel was contained in it, as delivered by the Saviour to the ancient inhabitants. Also that there were two stones in silver bows, and these stones fastened to a breastplate constituted what is called the Urim and Thummim, deposited with the plates, and the possession and use of these stones was what constituted seers in ancient or former times, and that God had prepared them for the purpose of translating the book. After telling me these things he commenced quoting the prophecies of the Old Testament, he first quoted part of the third chapter of Malachi; and he quoted also the fourth or last chapter of the same prophecy though with a little variation from the way it reads in our Bibles. Instead of quoting the first verse as reads in our books he quoted it thus, "For behold the day cometh that shall burn as an oven, and all the proud yea and all that do wickedly shall burn as stubble, for they that cometh shall burn them saith the Lord of hosts, that it shall leave them neither root nor branch," and again he quoted the fifth verse thus, "Behold I will reveal unto you the Priesthood by the hand of Elijah the prophet before the coming of the great and dreadful day of the Lord." He also quoted the next verse differently, "And he shall plant in the hearts of the children the promises made to the fathers, and the hearts of the children shall turn to their fathers, if it were not so the whole earth would be utterly wasted at his coming." In addition to these he quoted the eleventh chapter of Isaiah saying that it was about to be fulfilled. He quoted also the third chapter of Acts, twenty second and twenty third verses precisely as they stand in our New Testament. He said that that prophet was Christ, but the day had not yet come when "they who would not hear his voice should be cut off from among the people," but soon would come.

He also quoted the second chapter of Joel from the twenty eighth to the last verse. He also said that this was not yet fulfilled but was soon to be. And he further stated the fulness of the gentiles was soon to come in. He quoted many other passages of scripture and offered many explanations which cannot be mentioned here. Again he told me that when I got those plates of which he had spoken (for the time that they should be obtained was not yet fulfilled) I should not show them to any person, neither the breastplate with the Urim and Thummim only to those to whom I should be commanded to show them, if I did I should be destroyed. While he was conversing with me about the plates the vision was opened to my mind that I could see the place where the plates were deposited and that so clearly and distinctly that I knew the place again when I visited it.

The official version of Smith's 1823 encounter with an angel says he identified the angelic being as Moroni. However, the April 15, 1842 edition of the Times and Seasons *says Smith claimed the angel called himself Nephi. The 1851 edition of the* Pearl of Great Price *also states the angel's name was Nephi, not Moroni.*

contains a condition for the sale of the copyright. According to Page they were to sell the copyright to purchasers "if they would not harden their hearts." They say it was because of the Canadians' hard hearts that the copyright did not sell, and not because of Joseph Smith's lack of spiritual insight.

This excuse does not account for Smith's reply when confronted by his contemporaries and asked to give an explanation for the failure. If this condition were indeed true, why was Smith puzzled by the situation, asking the Lord concerning the matter, and then responding by saying:

> Some revelations are of God: some revelations are of man: and some revelations are of the devil. (*An Address to All Believers in Christ,* p. 31)

If there were indeed a condition for the sale, there would be no need for Smith to apologize or to attribute this revelation to the devil or the heart of man.

Smith also claimed the American Civil War "would be poured out upon all nations" (*Doctrine and Covenants,* 87:2). History shows this was not the case.

In 1832 Smith prophesied that a temple would be built in Independence, Missouri, "which temple shall be reared in *this* generation. For verily *this* generation shall not all pass away until an house shall be built unto the Lord" (*Doctrine and Covenants,* 84:4–5). To this day there is no such temple.

In 1835 Smith stated:

> It was the will of God that those who went to Zion, with the determination to lay down their lives, if necessary, should be ordained to the ministry, and go forth to prune the vineyard for the last time, or the coming of the Lord, which was nigh—even fifty-six years should wind up the scene. (*History of the Church,* 2:182)

This would place the second coming of Christ in 1891. Once again, Smith's prophecy was proven false.

Like a hereditary disease this trait was passed down to other church authorities. Brigham Young declared that by 1882 the Elders of the Mormon church would be thought of as kings on their thrones (*Journal of Discourses,* 4:40). He also said the Civil War would not free the slaves (*Journal of Discourses,* 10:250).

In 1886 Heber C. Kimball prophesied that Brigham Young would become the President of the United States (*Journal of Discourses*, 5:219).

Paul warns of false prophets in 2 Corinthians 11:13:

> For such are false apostles, deceitful workers, transforming themselves into the apostles of Christ.

In desperation Mormons grasp at any so-called prophecy that Smith might have made that *did* come to pass. But even this cannot prove he was a true prophet, for the Bible says even a false prophet can be right sometimes:

> If there arise among you a prophet, or a dreamer of dreams, and giveth thee a sign or a wonder, *and the sign or the wonder come to pass*, whereof he spake unto thee saying, let us go after other gods, which thou hast not known and let us serve them; Thou shalt not hearken unto the words of that prophet. . . . (Deuteronomy 13:1–3; italics added)

It would seem the writer of this passage had Joseph Smith in mind when he penned the words. The fourth chapter of the Book of Abraham reveals that Smith did indeed introduce other gods. One need only compare the characteristics of Joseph Smith's god with those describing the God of the Bible to know that he spoke of other gods.

Jeremiah 23:30–32 and 39–40 show what God thinks of people who prophesy falsely:

> Therefore, behold, I am against the prophets, saith the Lord, that steal my words every one from his neighbor. Behold, I am against the prophets, saith the Lord, that use their tongues, and say, He saith. Behold, I am against them that prophesy false dreams, saith the Lord, and do tell them, and cause my people to err by their lies, and by their lightness: yet I sent them not, nor commanded them: therefore, they shall not profit this people at all, saith the Lord. . . . Therefore, behold, I, even I, will utterly forget you, and I will forsake you, and the city that I gave you and your fathers, and cast you out of my presence: And I will bring an everlasting reproach upon you, and a perpetual shame, which shall not be forgotten.

Every prophecy of God will come to pass. All those who have been deceived by the words of Joseph Smith and other false prophets will for eternity regret having heard their names, and will hold them in reproach for the damnation that has come upon their souls for accepting a false gospel and not that of the true and living God.

37

Do you really think Joseph Smith would have suffered so much persecution and died a martyr if his claims were untrue?

It is highly possible for a person to die for something he knew in the beginning was not the truth. A lie, repeated often enough, becomes as truth to the teller. It appears that in order to cover up his first lie, Smith lied again; then to make the second lie appear as truth he lied again, and so on. Finally, having told the story so many times and having convinced so many of it, he believed it also. The Bible calls a person of this nature a reprobate. And the person, convinced of the validity of his story, will in some cases even die for it.

The idea that Joseph Smith died a martyr is a myth. Mormons compare Smith's death to that of the Savior and even say he went as a "lamb to the slaughter." The facts reveal something very different. Smith did not die willingly as the LDS church would have us believe. Smith obtained a smuggled pistol while in the jail at Carthage, and as the mob approached, he opened fire. Had his gun not misfired, he no doubt would have taken more with him into eternity. Volume seven of the *History of the Church* quotes John Taylor, an eyewitness to the act:

> He [Joseph Smith], however, instantly arose, and with a firm, quick step, and a determined expression of countenance, approached the door, and pulling the six-shooter left by Brother Wheelock from his pocket, opened the door slightly [of the jail cell] and snapped the pistol six successive times; only three of the barrels, however, were discharged. I afterwards understood that two or three

Carthage jail

While being incarcerated at Carthage jail, Smith was attacked by an angry mob and shot. While Mormons today hail him as a martyr, few are aware that he had a smuggled pistol and shot at his attackers, killing two of them.

were wounded by these discharges, two of whom, I am informed, died (p. 101).

John Taylor later became Mormonism's third prophet, following the death of Brigham Young in 1877.

While Mormons may rightly defend their prophet's act of self-defense, it is mendacious to say he died as a lamb led to the slaughter. To compare Smith's death to that of the Lord Jesus is far from the truth.

38

What about all the fruits of Mormonism?

Wherefore by their fruits ye shall know them. (Matthew 7:20)

To answer this question one needs to look at the fruits of Mormonism.

Mormons profess a plurality of gods, when the Bible plainly declares there is but one God.

They call the *Book of Mormon* "the everlasting gospel." Any gospel, no matter what it is called, is another gospel if it contradicts the message of the Bible.

Leaders of the Mormon church declare the Bible to be full of errors and not to be trusted.

Putting aside all the so-called accomplishments of Mormonism, all the "fruit" necessary to classify Smith as a false prophet was revealed in 1820 when he announced that he actually saw God. Both the Bible and the *Doctrine and Covenants* say this was not possible.

Brigham Young, also claimed by Mormons to be a prophet of God, gave many false prophecies as well.

A list of successes is not proof of authenticity. And though the Mormon will use theirs in an effort to prove their own authenticity, they will not acknowledge the accomplishments of other organizations.

The early Mormon church introduced polygamy, and to this day they believe they will practice it again in the hereafter (*Mormon Doctrine*, p. 578).

Utah is about 77% Mormon (according to the 1991–1992 LDS *Church Almanac*). And although their public relations department would have us believe otherwise, it is hardly the epitome of virtue. The same social ills that plague our nation as a whole are also found in Utah, and in some cases at even a higher rate.

In the 148 years following the founding of the Mormon church, they taught that Blacks were cursed by God.

The doctrine of "blood atonement," taught strongly by Brigham

Young, no doubt was a major factor in the slaughtering of some 130 immigrants at the Mountain Meadows in September 1857.

Mormons profess that their leaders are the only ones with the authority to speak the things of God, and that all others are in a state of apostasy. Despite this claim, their leaders have often contradicted one another, and many times even contradicted their standard works.

After close examination, the "fruits" of the LDS church are found to be tainted.

A challenge to all members of the Church of Jesus Christ of Latter-Day Saints

In the preceding pages I have sought to answer many of the questions often asked of me as a Christian. I would like to ask you if the Mormon faith can be questioned in a similar manner? I challenge you to answer the following questions. If Mormonism is as true as it claims to be, the following should not be hard to answer:

The doctrine of polygamy was abolished in 1890 with *The Manifesto*; the curse on Blacks was lifted in 1978. Why has the Mormon church changed their position on these and other issues when Alma 41:8 says, "the decrees of God are unalterable"?

Joseph Smith taught that a man could get closer to God by following the precepts found in the *Book of Mormon* (*Teachings of the Prophet Joseph Smith*, p. 194). Since marriage in a Mormon temple is a requirement for exaltation, why is it that this doctrine is not taught in the *Book of Mormon*? And why does this book fail to mention the plurality of gods, the word of wisdom, a heavenly mother, baptism for the dead, three degrees of glory, and other doctrines peculiar to the Mormon faith?

Can you prove that Brigham Young *did not* teach that Adam was God? And if he did teach that Adam was God, you must admit he taught false doctrine—which, according to the Bible, would make him a false prophet.

If you are worshiping the God of the Bible, why does your heavenly Father know of other gods, when the God of the Bible says in Isaiah 44:8 that there is no God besides Him?

Was Enoch 430 years old when he was translated, as told in *Doctrine and Covenants*, 107:49, and Moses 8:1; or was he 365 years old, as revealed on page 170 of the *Teachings of the Prophet Joseph Smith* and in Genesis 5:23?

The Bible teaches that a true believer has the witness of the Spirit that he is saved and ready for heaven. Are you certain that if you were to die today that you would be in the presence of the Lord?

2 Nephi 25:23 says you are saved by grace "after all you can do."

Have you done all you can do? How do you know if you have or have not done all you can do?

Eternity is too long and too final to regret having taken a person's word for the requirements of your salvation. I urge you to verify Mormonism's claims with those of the Bible. Don't trust your feelings or the experiences of others alone. Find out for yourself. Study the Word of God to discover the true condition of man and his need for a perfect Savior. Put your trust in the completed work of Jesus Christ alone.

Bibliography

Standard Mormon Works
Book of Mormon, 1830, 1908, 1963, and 1981 editions.
Doctrine and Covenants, 1981.
Pearl of Great Price, 1981.

Works Written by Mormons and/or Published by the LDS Church
Address to All Believers in Christ, An, David Whitmer, 1887.
Articles of Faith, The, James Talmage, 1982 ed. Published by the LDS church.
Comprehensive History of the Church, B. H. Roberts. BYU Press.
Divergent Paths of the Restoration, Steven Shields, 1982. Restoration Research.
Doctrines of Salvation, Joseph Fielding Smith, 1954. Deseret Publishing Co.
Early Mormonism and the Magic World View, D. Michael Quinn. Signature.
Evidences and Reconciliations, John Widtsoe, 1987. Bookcraft.
Gospel Through the Ages, The, Milton R. Hunter, 1945. Stevens & Wallis.
History of the Church. Deseret Publishing Co.
Jesus the Christ, James Talmage, 1915. Deseret News.
Joseph Smith—Seeker After Truth, John Widtsoe, 1951. *Deseret News*.
Journal of Discourses. Bookcraft Publishing Co.
Marvelous Work and a Wonder, A, LeGrand Richards, 1969. Deseret Publishing Co.
Mormon Corporate Empire, The, Heinerman & Shupe, 1985. Beacon Press.
Mormon Doctrine, Bruce McConkie, 1966. Bookcraft Publishing Co.
New Witness for Christ in America, A, Francis Kirkham, 1959. Utah Printing.
1989–1990 LDS Church Almanac. Deseret Publishing Co.
Seer, The, Orson Pratt, 1854.
Sure Foundation, A, 1988. Deseret Publishing Co.
Teachings of the Prophet Joseph Smith, Joseph Fielding Smith, 1977 ed.
Times and Seasons. Independence Press.

Christian Exegetical and Apologetic Works
Dictionary of Old Testament Words, Aaron Pick, 1977. Kregel Publishing Co.
Does the Bible Contradict Itself?, W. F. Arndt, 1955. Concordia Publishers.
Expository Dictionary of New Testament Words, An, Vine. Revell Publishing Co.
King James Version Defended, The, Dr. D. F. Hills, 1979. Eye Opener Publications.
Which Bible?, Dr. David O. Fuller, 1978, Grand Rapids International Publishing.
God in Three Persons, E. Calvin Beisner, 1984. Tyndale House Publishers.
Temple, The, Alfred Edersheim, 1976. Wm. B. Eerdman Publishing Co.

Scripture Index